EFFECTIVE PSYCHOTHERAPY FOR PATIENT AND THERAPIST

EFFECTIVE PSYCHOTHERAPY FOR PATIENT AND THERAPIST

Jules Meisler

PRAEGER

New York
Westport, Connecticut
London

Library of Congress Cataloging-in-Publication Data

Meisler, Jules.
    Effective psychotherapy for patient and therapist / by Jules
Meisler.
        p.   cm.
    Includes bibliographical references and index.
    ISBN 0–275–93985–5 (alk. paper)
    1. Psychotherapist and patient.   2. Psychotherapy.   I. Title.
    [DNLM: 1. Professional-Patient Relations. 2. Psychotherapy.
WM 420 M515e]
    RC480.8.M45   1991
    616.89′14—dc20
DNLM/DLC
for Library of Congress   91–2881

British Library Cataloguing in Publication Data is available.

Library of Congress Catalog Card Number: 91–2881
ISBN: 0–275–93985–5

First published in 1991

Praeger Publishers, One Madison Avenue, New York, NY 10010
An imprint of Greenwood Publishing Group, Inc.

Printed in the United States of America

The paper used in this book complies with the
Permanent Paper Standard issued by the National
Information Standards Organization (Z39.48–1984).

10 9 8 7 6 5 4 3 2 1

This book is dedicated to
Louis Booth

Contents

Introduction

Looking back, I realize that this book had its genesis in experiences during my two years in graduate school. I attended classes a few days and worked as a trainee in a social agency the other days of the week. During this time, both the school and the training supervisor were questioning me because I was not applying what I was taught in the classroom to actual situations. How was I going to tell these well-intentioned, more experienced, better-trained, better-educated people—full professors, mind you, people who had published books and articles—that most of what they were teaching and expecting me to use did not work? Social work interviewing has a large therapeutic component in its make-up. The social worker tries to help the person or family modify the emotions and feelings that interfere with relationships or the use of their environment. I was taught principles that did not tell me specifically and concretely what I should do. They were too vague. Today, I think an individual apprenticeship is needed which no school teaching psychotherapeutic techniques, then or now, can afford.

The only way I seemed to help people was by reacting to them as one human being to another. Even that did not work too well because too much of me became personally involved with what I was doing, and their lives became my life. I told them what to do and expected them to do it as if I were talking to myself. They rightly refused my demands.

After graduation in 1958, I worked in different social agencies for the next ten years, searching for a way to help people change emotionally so they could enjoy their lives. I tried a number of approaches I had heard of or read about. They started by telling me what to do in the beginning but then stopped working as the directions petered out. Many times they did not work because the theory behind the approach did not fit the person. I continued to work with people, as before, backing off from taking over their lives. Upset persons and families were relieved of their stress. They said they had benefited because they were not feeling as helpless and anxiety-ridden. I could not tell them that all we had done was to gain them some distance from the situation so they could see what they wanted to do; that the emotions and feelings which had gotten them into the mess were still there to get them into trouble again at a later time; that they were experiencing the calm between storms. And furthermore, I did not know how to help them modify their emotions and feelings.

In 1963 I began psychotherapy with Louis Booth, Ph.D., now deceased. The ideas I discussed in this book originated with Louis Booth. My contribution was to clarify and organize them. I am solely responsible for any confusions or distortions of his ideas.

By 1968 we had decided I was ready to go into private practice as a psychotherapist. Booth began teaching me the approach to psychotherapy he had used in my treatment. He had evolved the method because current practices in the field were not working very effectively. We called it many names, but the latest is character therapy since its basic aim is to enable the person to express the character he was born with as fully as possible.

The field of psychotherapy contains many theories but little direction on how to apply them. Except by trial and error, which could be harmful, the therapist and patient do not know if the theory and approach used fit the person. Therefore, a method of treatment is needed in which therapist and patient have some idea of what they are trying to do, how they will do it, and some way to tell them if they are on the right track. This book describes such an approach to treatment in which both the therapist and patient have defined jobs and know why they are doing them.

Although character theory contains much that is familiar, we use this material within the context of a different philosophy.

The difficulty for both patient and therapist in doing effective work is that no concrete step-by-step process enables human beings to resolve emotional problems. Something is needed that tells the therapist and patient, "First you do A, then depending on the reaction to A you do B or C, and contingent on those results you go to D, E," and so on. Instead, there are a series of generic directions applicable to almost any theory, such as:

1. Establish a therapeutic relationship.
2. Involve the patient in the treatment process.
3. Try to uncover the problem causing emotions and feelings and help the patient to resolve them.

No theory tells the therapist how to do these things concretely and specifically.

All theories of human behavior are unproven and based on undefined fundamentals. There are no generally accepted definitions of a therapeutic relationship, treatment involvement, emotions and feelings, and many other psychological phenomena. Even so, the patient must comprehend these terms and understand how they are applied. The more the person understands the therapeutic situation, the better she can help the therapist to help her. If therapists do not understand the basics of their discipline, they cannot explain their application to the patient and so enable her to effectively participate in her treatment.

Many times, no satisfactory definition or description of psychological phenomena is available. Where this is so, I have considered what the phenomenon does. It is the same as electricity: We don't know what it is but we can talk about what it does. In this sense we approach ill-defined fundamentals.

Psychic phenomena are dynamic. They are never still: motion is their essence. The concepts discussed in this book are meant to be equally dynamic. If they appear static, I have not adequately described them.

I assume that general readers have some psychology background. My purposes in writing this book were as follows.

First, to give the intelligent layperson in therapy a full enough idea of what should happen in treatment so that she can ask her therapist what the two of them are doing, how, and why. The patient is the equal of the therapist in the treatment process. The only difference between them is the therapist knows better than the patient how to look for the emotions and feelings that need modification.

Second, to inform the intelligent layperson considering entering psychotherapy of what is involved so he can decide if it is what he wants.

Third, to give therapists a way to apply and validate any theory that accepts the existence of the unconscious. This method tries to reduce the anxiety all therapists live with by suggesting what to do, when, and how, as they encounter various problems in working effectively. It reduces the anxiety of the patient who can sense the therapist's insecurity and inability to cope with emotional upset. The more relaxed both therapist and patient are, the more effectively they can work. When overcome by emotion, they achieve very little. It is like the prize fighter who fights better if he is a little angry, drawing on his energy in a controlled way, but swings wildly when his anger overwhelms him. This approach enables the therapist to constantly validate the theory she is using and keep in touch with what is happening between her and her patient. Therapists who want to learn this method need the intellectual and emotional understanding gained by hands-on experience discussed in an individual training program.

The whole structure of treatment described in this book is on the level of horse-and-buggy transportation. I hope it will lead some gifted psychological mechanic to create a better method, equivalent to the internal combustion engine.

1

The Beginning of the Therapeutic Situation

THE THERAPIST'S BACKGROUND

Therapists are born, not made. They have an ability to use an innate extra sensitivity to another person's emotional state for the benefit of that person. Education and training help them organize and use what they already have but does not increase their therapeutic aptitude.

One of the therapist's talents is the ability to be passive, to be quiet, listen, and let the other person's imagination make him over. As the patient talks with him, the patient imputes certain reactions and behaviors to the therapist which may or may not exist. She should tell the therapist what she is thinking and feeling. From the distorted images the patient has about him, the therapist can deduce what a part of the problem is. While watching what unfolds, the therapist must live with increased anxiety because he will not understand what is happening for some time.

Therapists should know about human behavior in areas other than psychology. They must be sensitive to language, what is said, when and how it is said. They should know about art, religion, crafts, philosophy, popular attitudes, literature, any kind of meaningful human activity. Such knowledge gives them the material they need to create explanations of their patients' behavior. For example, a therapist could think an elderly patient's behavior is reminiscent of Shakespeare's King Lear and from that derive a theory that explains what is happening with the gentleman.

On the one hand, therapists are not supposed to expect anything of their patients. On the other hand, they do expect their patients to pay for treatment, to truthfully report all of their thoughts and feelings, to trust their therapist, and to keep appointments. Therapists must be detached enough from themselves to be aware of their reactions and also maintain a professional distance with those patients who do not meet these expectations. Psychotherapy may become necessary for therapists who are frequently unaware of their feelings and react personally to patients.

Therapists must feel comfortable while depending on their patients for help in doing psychotherapy. For some time, therapists must explain what they need their patients to do so that effective therapy can happen. In the beginning, the therapist follows the person's choice of topics discussed and works in the explanations as opportunities arise. This topic is expanded in this and subsequent chapters.

Therapists should have experienced many different kinds of pain so that they are sensitive to the nuances when patients talk about their pain. A nuance is the delicate shade of difference a common experience has for a particular person. Sensitivity to nuances tells the patient the therapist understands him. Any therapist can understand what a divorced person is going through as the patient reports his thoughts and feelings. The divorced therapist grasps more of what the person is undergoing emotionally and responds more knowingly and precisely to the patient's feelings because he has had a similar experience. This does not preclude the therapist's ability, in either case, to help the patient.

Because the mind-body problem is unresolved, therapists need to bring the following philosophical attitudes to their psychotherapeutic work or acquire them after they begin seeing patients. We discuss these at greater length in Chapter 5.

1. There is no cure, in the medical sense of removing a lesion. Patients are helped to understand their emotional conditions so they can

cope by themselves and live with a greater degree of comfort. They are helped to adapt to life with what they have available to them.

2. There is no basic problem in the sense of a central source from which all of a patient's upset comes. The person and the emotional difficulty are one and the same. The problem is diffused throughout the person's emotional make-up.

3. Cause and effect do not apply in psychotherapy because they cannot be located and separated from each other. The effects of important life experiences are extremely complicated and pervasive and are interrelated with parents, siblings, school, the outside world generally, and the person's genetic endowment. What happens to a person as she goes through an emotional experience is what is important.

4. A patient's history does not equal the person. The whole individual is greater than the sum of all his parts.

PATIENTS IN THERAPY

The Background of the Patient

The beginning of psychotherapy starts as a necessity but should end as a choice. People should enter psychotherapy when they are in pain and at the end of their rope. The person must have a problem he cannot live with because it is destroying him. He must have realized something is wrong, tried everything he could think of, and found that nothing helped. He is compelled to enter treatment and then find his anxiety is reduced so that his mind is not frozen. He can begin making choices.

Candidates for Psychotherapy

Psychotherapy can help only those persons who have the ability to endure pain. People who live on the basis of pleasure a great deal, who are controlled by it, who find it very difficult to say no to themselves, cannot be helped because effective treatment involves deprivation and pain. Substance abusers who have not withdrawn from drugs cannot use therapy because when it hurts too much they increase their drug usage. One of the hardest things in the world is to say no to life. Yes is always easier. Living on the basis of pleasure precludes coming to decisions.

People simply hold on to everything, both the present situation and that which gives relief from the present situation. Nothing gets resolved. An example of this is the unhappily married man who wants to live with his mistress but does not leave his wife because it would diminish his income.

Some people cannot be helped because they are so successful in manipulating themselves and others. If this is taken away, they have nothing else left. These people do not feel enough pain to make them want to change. They avoid any introspection about themselves by keeping themselves busily involved in trying to actualize their fantasies. They cannot permit reduction of their need to fantasize and find enough pleasure in reality instead. Such people cannot stop manipulating themselves and others long enough to let themselves feel their emotional difficulties and learn that, in part, these problems are due to themselves. They are incapable of stepping back from themselves and seeing what they are like.

Therapists have to face the fact that there are some people they cannot help. Sometimes the therapists do not know enough. Other times, some people are unreachable for all kinds of reasons. If therapists can accept this limit, they can work in a more relaxed manner. They can let patients know of their limitations in such a way that patients have to make choices. Does the patient elect to be controlled by her illness or her desire for health?

Candidates should have enough intelligence that their curiosity can be aroused as a way to involve them in their treatment. Generally, these patients are inflexible, highly intellectual, well-informed, and curious. The better the therapist explains what the two of them are doing, the more the patient becomes curious and interested intellectually. At some point, without being aware of it, the patient crosses over into the emotional. She becomes excited about the ideas she is discussing with the therapist. It may be the first time in her life she can talk with someone about her ideas. Eventually, she learns that many of her ideas are defensive, to protect herself from something. Her talking is not an explanation but a way of confusing things for herself. She will deny this revelation at first but come to accept it as the therapist explains the unconscious that contains many motivating emotions and feelings of which she was unaware.

The therapist has to know how the patient escapes from her emotions and feelings and try to stop it without wasting too much treatment time. For instance, a long-standing physical condition coming from an emotional problem—a conversion reaction—is pretty difficult to do much about using the known methods of helping. The therapist is banging her head against a stone wall. I do not know if the character therapy method of doing psychotherapy can help people afflicted with schizophrenia, paranoia, or manic states. Many depressed people have responded well.

One of the implications of a symptom is that it gives therapists some predictability because a symptom is a piece of behavior that became distorted in the past. When therapists can discover the conditions that made the distortions necessary, they can compare these with present situations. If the similarity is close, the past behavior tells therapists quite a bit about how these persons behave now. Based on the present small differences of feeling and behavior, the therapist gets an idea of what treatment can accomplish. Is the patient more aware of his feelings? Is his behavior as compulsive?

Before anything can begin to happen, patients and therapists have to see if they can work with each other. The personalities involved and their style of working greatly affect what they can accomplish. Patient and therapist study and sense much about each other via nonlogical methods that determine the outcome of treatment. Therapists must respond to nonverbal communication as this is one way patients know practitioners are with them in feeling. Sigmund Freud faced his patients with his self, whereas, most of his disciples face their patients with Freud's theories. Communication dies when the interview becomes one human being talking to the other as a theory.

Frequently, therapists go by their feelings because many of the criteria for a good psychotherapy candidate are unknown. Nonetheless, some criteria include:

1. A therapist who does not think she can help a patient to arrive at a more comfortable way to live should not attempt treatment.
2. A therapist must not assume that he knows the person's potential. Many times he does not and may write off the patient too soon.

3. A patient must not be too set in her ways. This is determined by giving the person time and seeing how she changes.
4. A patient must have a sense of self that gives him enough security to try to be himself.

Working in Depth

Many therapists believe that only as they talk about the id, the ego, and the superego in some form or another can they help patients. This is false. There is an unconscious, and therefore, something very deep is always happening. The particular concept of the unconscious the therapist is using may or may not apply to an individual patient. The unconscious is known by what it does, not by what it is thought to be. Therefore, therapists should look at what the unconscious is doing.

Therapists should start on the surface with behavior. Behavior is not superficial if therapists look at what it stands for—if a connection can be made between behavior, an outside object, and the patient's self. The connection tells therapists something about the unconscious that they cannot know or see directly. It is the same as when a person goes outside on a windy day. Although the wind is invisible, he can see the effect it has.

Therapists can talk about working on the surface but not about working in depth. The patient cannot comprehend emotional depth except as a word, such as a deep dive, a deep hole. Therapists should not use the words *deep* or *depth*, if ever, until after they illustrate it. They confuse patients and give them a sense of importance they should not have: "See, I'm different. I'm deep."

Depth can be illustrated by the patient who all of a sudden makes an association. He dreams, for example, of something in the past that he has not thought about in 15 years and today, as it came back to him, he shared it with the therapist. The therapist says, "You see, if you weren't here, you wouldn't have thought of it. But you did think of it, so what?" The therapist is questioning how to use that association to explain the current situation. The association has some relationship to the present, otherwise the patient would not have thought of it. This is deep in the emotions.

Some patients cannot be worked with in depth. By working

in depth, I mean frequently triggering reactions from the unconscious. With such patients, therapists should stay on the surface as much as possible. Therapists should not work in depth with patients if they believe:

1. That it would be destructive either to the patient or others to really know what motivates her.

2. That if they worked intensively with a patient they would not know what to do after awhile.

3. That the patient is emotionally fragile, that is, he cannot cope with much anxiety or pain.

4. That the patient did not have healthy models to pattern herself after while growing up. Treatment can erode the pathological behavior the person modeled herself after but there must be a residue in those models that the patient can hold onto. Otherwise, the patient is left with feeling she is nothing. This a developmental stage the therapist cannot make up for now.

5. That the patient does not have enough emotional fat to live off of as illusions are destroyed. The person must have had enough positive experiences in his life to draw on to sustain him during painful, deprived periods of treatment. He must not be left emotionally impoverished. It takes time for the therapist to know if the patient has enough emotional fat.

With such patients, therapists should simply try to get them functioning and be available to start their motors again when they return in the future. Each return by the patient gives the therapist a chance to see if work in depth can be tried.

Generally, a patient exhibiting much resistance is a warning to the therapist not to work in depth. Resistance is created by the patient's perception, usually unconscious, that somehow the topic under discussion is dangerous. The function of resistance is to protect the patient from danger. The therapist must respect the patient's fear that she can't cope with the feelings being triggered by the discussion. This does not apply, however, in the situation where the patient is putting up a great deal of resistance but every once in a while opens up a little emotionally. Such a patient is fighting to retain his character armor, his defenses. The occasional opening tells the therapist to continue banging away at the character armor because one of these days it will crack open. (I discuss character armor in Chapter 2.)

Early Aggression

In the beginning, most patients want to put the therapist on the spot one way or another. It is their way of asserting themselves. Patients feel diminished and insignificant because they had to seek out help. In each instance, the attempt is different but its purpose is to reduce the therapist's stature. The practitioner must enable the person to feel she has not lost anything.

Vestiges

Patients come into therapy with the idea they can find in the present what they did not have in the past. This is not possible. They are trying to recreate in the present what, at most, can only be a vestige of the past. What they wanted in the past they wanted as a child. The patient is now an adult and must have it on an adult level. What they are looking for is further removed from becoming a possibility because the patient's current emotional distortions prevent her from recognizing what the past was or what she really wants.

To find out what patients want, therapists have to animate their backgrounds by having them talk about their experiences and how they felt about what happened, by having them relive their experiences. What did they think and feel then? What kind of fantasies did they have as children and adolescents? What might they be looking for now? By comparing past and present wants, the patient sees what he is looking for and can or cannot get.

Special Situations

Duress

When a patient has been pressured into beginning psychotherapy, the therapist has to counteract the duress the person feels. The practitioner should give the person a chance to decide if he wants to come again after the first interview.

Marital and Parent-Child Problems

In a marital situation, the therapist should first see the spouse who made the contact and then the other one, each individually. The initiating spouse who wants to talk about the situation feels more free to do so if seen alone. She feels slighted if the therapist tries to bypass her to see the other spouse first. Usually the other spouse is not doing anything because he is reluctant to seek help with the marriage. Whoever calls first may not become the patient but the therapist can clarify the situation and adjust for this later on. In the beginning, the therapist must learn enough to know where to start.

In dealing with a parent-child problem, the therapist should have individual interviews with each parent and the child so that all feel free to say whatever they want. Children should be mature enough to carry on a conversation with the therapist, usually not younger than ten. The child calls for an appointment after the therapist has seen each parent.

When everyone in either situation has been seen, the therapist has to decide whether to let them know of her treatment recommendations in a group or individually. The practitioner has to consider what effect the reasons for the recommendations might have on each member of the family. Sometimes the therapist's decision to work with a particular person is taken to mean that this individual is the cause of all the trouble.

Contact with Others

Once the initial sessions have been completed, therapists should try to avoid contact with any other members of the patient's family or other significant people except under very specific and carefully selected circumstances. Patients fear the therapist cannot keep what they said confidential when they see someone else and sometimes become jealous as well, claiming the therapist likes the other person better. Therapists must know why they are seeing a relative or significant other and the pitfalls and dangers involved before they agree to see them.

Sometimes it is important to determine to what degree the patient understands her behavior in a real concrete situation, such as the family. The therapist can check that by meeting with the family in the office to get information about the patient's behavior. This has nothing to do with treating the family or facilitating communication.

CREATING THE THERAPEUTIC SITUATION

In the beginning the therapist:

1. Gets an idea of how much time the patient needs and expands first sessions to two hours or longer, if necessary. As many subsequent lengthy sessions follow as are needed to reduce the anxiety the patient feels.

2. Listens, except for clarifying questions, and does not try to drain the patient dry of his story.

3. Gets information from the patient only if ready to use it then and there; does not try to get a history unless she can relate it to the person's present experiences. This gives the patient an idea of how the therapist will use what she gives her.

4. Has the patient realize that this is a team approach. If the person does not give the therapist something to work with, nothing happens. Whatever is accomplished, the patient gets at least 50 percent of the credit.

5. Helps the patient to discuss comfortably whether the patient wants to enter treatment.

Reducing Anxiety in the Patient

The Psychotherapeutic Road Map

Someone who has not had the experience cannot understand the turmoil people undergo while waiting for the first interview to start. Patients are in a heightened state of anxiety, not knowing what will happen, mulling over the problems that brought them to the therapist. Somehow talking will straighten them out. But how? Talk about what? At the same time, they doubt if anyone can help them.

On a table in my waiting room, a sign on a small pile of paper reads "Please Take One." Patients pick up this sheet:

Your Psychotherapeutic Road Map
Before going on a trip, it is helpful to look at a map because it gives

you an idea of where you are going and how you are to get there. It gives you a feeling of security and reduces anxiety. An example of anxiety is when you wake up in the dark with a start, terrified: you do not know where you are. You turn on the light, see your hotel room, and remember—you are on vacation. Psychotherapy is like a trip. It is a way to get to a more satisfying life. The purpose of this psycho-therapeutic road map is to shed some light on psychotherapy and help you feel comfortable.

As a human being, you are as unique as your fingerprints. You are not exceptional, however, in having human problems. Psychologically, a human problem is an incorrect, painful response to inner and outer pressures. It should be examined and corrected much like a physical problem. The important difference is that in the treatment of a physical problem you are mostly worked *on*: in this office you are worked *with*. Your cooperation determines whether therapy will be a success or failure.

Psychotherapy neither adds to nor subtracts from what you already have. Like a windshield wiper helping you to see more clearly and react more realistically to what you see, psychotherapy helps to clear your mind. One patient's definition of psychotherapy, based on his experi-ence, may help to remove some misconceptions. He said, "Therapy is like putting a jigsaw puzzle together. You lay all of your thoughts and all of your feelings out on the table, cut them up in pieces and then put them back together where they belong."

The purpose of psychotherapy is to enable you to make intelligent use of your emotions. Then you have reached your destination. You use your emotions instead of your emotions using you. An example of this is the person who becomes stronger when he becomes angry, but loses his strength when his anger overwhelms him.

Untreated emotional problems lead to using life destructively. Treated emotional problems can lead to using life constructively.

Please ask any questions you may have, big or small, and I will try to answer them. You will being helping me to help you better. Any question that concerns you is important and of interest to me.

Best wishes for a successful psychotherapeutic trip!

At first, the title does not mean much and neither does the text. It says something about asking questions, which is strange because they thought the therapist would ask them questions. They feel safer asking questions because they cannot give wrong answers and make fools of themselves or touch on things they do not want to talk about yet. They try to read the "road map" again. It seems a little clearer. They think, "I don't know what it's all about, but I have a feeling the therapist does, and that's a relief."

The psychotherapeutic road map tries to relieve some of the difficulties met at the very beginning of treatment. It empowers patients to feel confident without reducing the effectiveness of the therapist. It takes some time before the patients understand that talking freely is one of the goals of psychological treatment. Meanwhile, they need to observe the therapist/stranger in front of them and to talk without becoming too personal. With the encouragement from the road map, patients ask questions and observe their therapist's reactions. They commit themselves to treatment based on their personal observations and intuition.

The Patient Needs to Know the Therapist

At the very beginning of the first interview, the therapist explains that he will do the talking and the patient is to study him. The therapist further explains he will try to spell out, roughly, what the patient's problem is and what he will do about it. This is the quickest way the individual gets to know the therapist. If the patient knows what kind of person she is talking to and what to expect, her anxiety is reduced and she can be more relaxed and open with the therapist.

The Patient's and Therapist's Jobs

Sometimes a person has such a need to talk that the best thing the therapist can do is just listen and explain the patient's jobs at another time. Otherwise, the patient then learns she will have two jobs to do all through treatment. One of these jobs is to ask questions. The questions asked tell the therapist what is important to the patient, what needs to be discussed. Questioning gives the interview a direction. The therapist makes one of three responses to patients' questions:

1. Answers the question in a way that opens up the subject for further discussion.
2. Tells the patient he does not know, if that is the case.
3. Tells the patient if he does not think it is a good idea to answer the question.

The patient's second job is to correct the therapist. As they begin talking, the therapist lets the patient know any reactions, feelings, or ideas he has about what is happening between them. It is a way to discuss the impression the patient is making on the therapist. However, it carries the danger of the therapist making an error because human beings are complex and take a long time, if ever, to know. In correcting the therapist, both of them learn what is actually going on or that neither one knows what is happening. If the patient says to the therapist, "No, it is not A, as you say, but B", then they can discuss it, see if they agree it is B or decide that their understanding of what is happening remains an unknown. Agreement on B does not mean they have fully caught what is happening. They are saying, "Based on what we are aware of, this is what we think is going on, subject to further revision as we learn more."

At this time the therapist explains that his job is to summarize at the end what happened in each session. The purpose of summarizing is to pull the session into a tight package so that the patient can think about it afterward. In this way, treatment continues after the session is over. Occasionally, as a session is summarized, it triggers a flash of insight. Patients are instructed to interrupt and tell the therapist the insight before it is lost. (I discuss summarizing at greater length in Chapter 4.)

Eventually, the therapist exhausts the subject of jobs. At that point he explains that it is all right for the two of them to sit quietly and study each other if neither one has anything more to say. From here on, the therapist proceeds strictly on intuition. At some point in this process the patient feels she knows the therapist well enough and begins talking. The therapist then listens.

The Most Important Person in the Room

Therapists do not have to say a thing about their interest in, respect for, or concern about their patients. Their attitude must say it. Therapists are there for the needs of patients and that is what patients have to feel.

The patient leads the discussion and the therapist follows. They talk about what the patient wants to bring up. The therapist can guide the direction of the discussion toward a subject. If the patient says no to the topic, the only thing the therapist can do is to look at why it was refused. The therapist cannot go into the subject without the patient's agreement. Many times discussion of the patient's reasons for not wanting to talk about a particular topic frees the person to do so and uncovers unsuspected problems. Patients must feel they are in control of the situation. The only limitation is they cannot dictate how the therapist does therapy.

Initial Conceptualizing

During the opening sessions, the therapist helps the patient to think about how he sees himself. The therapist may disagree with the person's picture of himself, but does not challenge the patient. Therapists should be aware that for some time they will be dealing with psychological truth, the concept that what the patient says to be true is true, even when it is not so. It is what the patient needs to believe is true. A conceptualization is reassuring to the patient. Even if it is wrong, being able to think about and understand the situation enables the patient not to feel so helpless because he is doing something. Discussing the conceptualization with the therapist makes the patient feel understood and not so alone with his anxiety. In doing his own conceptualizing, the patient finds it easier to accept the implications of his thinking. He does not feel as if the therapist is imposing her ideas on him.

The Danger of Too-Comfortable Patients

The therapist should control the degree of anxiety patients are experiencing, increasing or reducing it as necessary. When they become too comfortable, patients begin to think they are "cured." The ever-present resistance to therapy causes them to think of stopping before they have even begun. The therapist should counteract this by frequently reminding patients why they are in treatment.

Recording Sessions

With the patient's permission, the therapist tapes all interviews beginning with the first session. The practitioner explains that she will listen to the recording later. If she feels something was touched on that should be looked at further, she will bring it up at another session. Additionally, therapists can use the tape recorder to help patients learn what they are feeling. (I describe the use of the tape recorder in Chapter 4.) Although the tape recorder is not used as an intervention in the beginning, there are exceptions, depending on the therapist's judgment. If the patient finds the request to tape record too anxiety-producing, the therapist should drop it for the time being.

Words and Their Associations

Therapists should use neutral words. For instance, I would not use the word *religion* when talking with a patient because for me it has an abstract and very often ominous association. It may have the same connotation for the patient. Negative associations can make a person end treatment prematurely.

Therapists should also avoid professional jargon. Both should use simple everyday language and talk as specifically and concretely as possible. This is to prevent misunderstandings and hiding of feelings in a smoke screen of words.

Definitions

Definitions can be given or asked for when either therapist or patient is not sure of what the other one is talking about. A definition is not fixed and static as it is in a dictionary. In psychotherapy, definitions are constantly changed to fit different circumstances and people. It is not Humpty-Dumpty's approach in Lewis Carroll's *Through the Looking Glass* in which a word meant whatever he said it meant. A definition is adapted dynamically for use in a particular situation. For example, *frustration* is defined in the *Dictionary of Psychology* by J. P. Chaplin as "1, blockage or thwarting of goal directed behavior; 2, an unpleasant state of tension, anxiety, and heightened sympathetic activity resulting from blockage or thwarting."[1] For patients who prevent themselves from getting what they want, I define their frustration as "Insisting on eating your favorite soup with a spoon that has a hole in it." Every definition must include a symbol with a strong emotional appeal to the patient so that it is therapeutically useful.

HOW PATIENTS ENTER THE THERAPEUTIC SITUATION

Patients Have Much to Accept

Patients must help therapists assist them if they are to learn how to cope with their problems and, eventually, live their own lives. Therapists can tell patients what material is needed and where to look for it. They ask patients to do certain things in a session to uncover what they are feeling. Therapists give people chances to try doing some of the interventions. They must have the patience to tolerate their difficulty in learning to do what is requested of them. Patients must feel that they and their therapists are a team. If one side does not do their part, nothing happens.

Distrust of the Therapist

Patients are ashamed to admit they do not trust their therapists. How can they feel that way about professionals they are paying to help them? They must come to realize that because of the negative life experiences which brought them into treatment they are suspicious in any situation and should discuss their fears whenever necessary. If they feel they have been lied to by people they trusted, why should they expect differently of their therapists? A sign of increasing trust is when patients are able to tell their therapists how they feel about them. Therapists have to be open emotionally, yet professional, giving patients time to get to know and trust them.

The Patient's Two Jobs

It is not easy for patients to ask questions. Sometimes they are in such pain and confusion that they cannot bear thinking about their situation to formulate a question. There may be an unconscious need to keep the situation as it is. Asking questions puts patients in a new and strange position for them—having power—and they are not comfortable using it. Patients need to feel their therapists are human like them before they feel free to ask questions. The biggest stumbling block is that patients sense that by asking questions they are revealing a great deal of themselves. The patient's question usually gives the therapist a look into the problem. Questions such as, "Why am I afraid to be alone?" begin to tell therapists what is bothering their patients, what they want.

Once patients have accepted the importance of questioning, they can apply it to themselves. They begin questioning what they think, feel, and do, thereby increasing their awareness of themselves and others. Both therapists and patients begin to feel futile if practitioners do not realize and point out specific indications of patients becoming more aware of how they and the people around them are feeling. In other words, change has begun. Not much will have happened emotionally, but the patient's awareness is changed. To other people this is an imperceptible difference. Calling attention to this encourages patients to involve themselves further in their treatment.

Questions are a way to think and talk about the unthinkable because patients are considering possibilities not facts. Spouses can wonder about divorce but freeze if it is to become an actuality. It is a tentative "Should I divorce him?", rather than a definite, "I will divorce him." Persons have room to move back and forth, for and against, when an action is approached as a question.

In the beginning, it is easier for patients to correct their therapists. They already have some impressions as to what their problems are and are looking for someone with whom they may safely discuss those ideas. The concepts they discuss also give therapists some inkling of their problems. Adolescent patients talking about parents who are too easygoing may be revealing desires to have limits placed on their behavior. The therapist's open reception of their corrections encourages patients to make other corrections as the need arises.

Patient Reporting

Therapists explain dreams and fantasies, discussed in Chapter 4, to patients. They ask patients to bring dreams and fantasies to an interview for discussion, along with questions, observations, ideas, complaints, and confusions. Using all this material is a way of finding out what patients are feeling on conscious and unconscious levels. Patients soon accept that the reporting of these phenomena enables their therapists to help them. On the other hand, knowing they are revealing much of themselves, patients tend to resist bringing in this material until they feel safe with their therapists.

Accepting the Unconscious

Patients have to experience the unconscious to accept its existence. They have to feel it as a force over which they have no control. Many opportunities to demonstrate the existence of the unconscious occur within an interview. Some of these are patients forgetting what was just said or what happened in the previous session, verbal slips, misunderstandings, blanking out, or becoming aware of a feeling they did not know was there.

Therapists must find different ways to discuss the unconscious, which is nothing but a word to most people. The more ways therapists find of talking about the unconscious in terms of their patients' experiences, the better they understand the unconscious and what needs to be done therapeutically.

The unconscious can be compared to the fermentation of beer. People think they select what they should do and how they should live, but that may not be so at all. Is it possible that emotions and feelings ferment and determine a person's thinking? If so, thinking is equivalent to the foam on a glass of beer. The person acting only on the basis of thought is like someone drinking foam instead of beer.

WHAT THE THERAPIST IS TRYING TO DO

Therapists try to involve patients emotionally and intellectually in their treatment, making emotional modification possible while avoiding psychosis. The most important thing therapists do is to prepare patients for psychotherapy. Preparation is of such great significance that I have devoted all of Chapter 2 to discussing how to do it.

Making Things Happen

The idea that eventually patients will talk about what they and their therapists want to know is both correct and incorrect. It is more often a wish than a reality. In due course, everything happens: we are born, we live, we die. The unconscious moves on its course no matter what a therapist does. One of the therapist's jobs is to make it move sooner. To do this, therapists have to jolt patients out of their ruts. By using interventions, therapists and patients find out what they need to know sooner than 10 or 15 years from now. This is discussed at greater length in Chapter 4.

An explanation or interpretation has to be implemented, otherwise it is useless. It, too, is an intervention because it triggers a reaction. Assuming it is correct, once a therapist has an idea in the back of her mind, the problem becomes how and when to use it to make things happen.

Making Abstract Language More Effective

The Use of Abstractions

How abstract language is used is very important in the character theory approach. A major principle is always connect the word to a reality. Take the term *addiction*. An addiction is the inability to resist habitually giving one's self up to a drug, state of mind, or person. It is a psychological force that comes out of a particular reality. When patients keep using the word *addiction*, they are inclined to overlook the reality out of which the addiction arises. They do not think of the physical and emotional conditions that bring on the behavior labeled an addiction. Therapists must help patients connect their talking to reality.

Concretizing Abstract Theory

What is psychology to the therapist is sometimes nonsense to the patient. Psychology is the practitioner's preconceived notion of the patient as described by the theories the therapist believes. Until the theory becomes real, it is just so much nonsense to the patient.

When therapists apply a theory they really do not know what their patients think or feel. They find out by applying a theory and seeing what happens. Patients' reactions to their therapists' behavior are filled with details that confirm or deny the theory.

Their responses concretize the theory, stimulate further thinking, and trigger more emotions.

Patients may believe they are burying therapists in trivia but therapists are interested in such ordinary details because they describe how the facts came about. Trivia are the nuances of unconscious expression. What is said and done, when and how, reflects what is going on inside the person. Patients need to know the commonplace occurrence is important. When therapists get their patients to give trivia instead of just facts, they begin to understand how the patients' unconsciouses are working and can demonstrate this to them. This begins to make the theory real. When therapists do not take the platitudinous and the obvious for granted, they can understand and use trivia effectively. The therapist who asked patients what they meant by describing themselves as upset got descriptions of fear and anger that were therapeutically useful. "I was really upset. I wanted to hit him, but couldn't bring myself to do it."

From Abstract Language to Concrete Experience

Therapists must make a transition when they go to concrete experience from abstract language or vice versa, otherwise their patients cannot follow and understand them. An example is the patient who talked about dropping a friend who was a great influence in his life; he believed he would be finished with him. In this instance, I talked about how grease from fixing a car so worked its way into my hands that I had to wash a number of times before I could get it out. Becoming abstract, I pointed out to the patient his relationship with his friend had affected his psyche similarly. The patient could then make the connection that his relationship with his friend will have to be dealt with over and over again until it comes out of his psyche as the grease came out of my hands.

Concretizing can be overdone just as being abstract can. At such a point, the therapist should become abstract. A patient of mine visualized anxiety as a group of running motors not connected to anything. He felt secure with motors because he was an engineer. He could avoid awareness of his fear by reacting to the motor as a motor, not seeing it as a symbol of his fear at all. I became abstract and talked about how he copes with fear and anxiety by treating them as "a sound and fury, signifying nothing", that is, trying to ignore them.

Establishing the Beginning Therapeutic Framework

Interview Length and Frequency

Beginning with the first session, therapists experiment to find the most effective combination of interview length and frequency. The question the practitioner tries to answer is, "How much time, how often, does this person need so we can work effectively?" After the initial reduction of anxiety, an interview should not run over an hour—even if the patient requests it, unless the therapist judges an exception to this rule is necessary—because a patient's attention span generally lasts for only an hour. In lengthy interviews, patients are confused in the first hour or so because they do not feel an inner pressure to bring out what they have to. Their attitude is "Well, I have time." Usually, the last 15 or 20 minutes of a regular hourly interview are the most fruitful. Therapists should increase the number of visits per week if their patients' pain becomes too much for them or if they remain closed up. The sessions should be lengthened if anxiety needs to be reduced.

Aside from these rules of thumb, practitioners must let things happen; they must not pour the coffee before it is pretty well percolated. Even though talking is the way patients release the emotional rust in which they are encased, therapists need to have an idea of how much rust exists. The tendency of most therapists is to start cleaning right away. Because the rust was collected by nature, therapists should wait to see what nature can do once they have triggered forces that work on the rust.

Direction

Direction is the therapist's view of the patient. It should come early in the contact and is derived mainly from intuition. It is a tentative theory that is easily replaced if it turns out not to fit. Direction is a vague approach to treatment when therapists are not clear what they are trying to accomplish in the long run.

Unless therapists have specific approaches, especially in difficult cases, they will not have any idea if they are getting somewhere.

In arriving at a direction, therapists have the professional responsibility to decide what is bad, not good, for patients. Therefore, therapist direction is a going away from a negative, not a going to a positive. In the beginning of treatment, people compulsively direct their attention to the problems. When they become more aware of their emotions and feelings, patients move away from the problems but therapists do not know their goals.

A goal is, to a degree, a specific place both therapist and patient are going toward. With a goal the therapist knows with much clarity, if not exactly, what she is headed for. A direction will carry a therapist only so far. If she has not evolved a goal, she will get lost. Most of the time if the therapist has a direction, a goal emerges. Coming out of the person's needs, the goal is decided by the patient, not the therapist. When the therapist has an approximately accurate direction and the patient has confidence in the therapist, the goal will come out of what goes on between the two of them.

Paleontological Psychology. In this work therapists never get enough facts to really know their patients. They don't know each person's past because it would take years to talk about an individual's childhood. Therapists need to know something about their patients' backgrounds as one way of finding out if the patients' behavior is pathological; that is, if it is based on disappointing past experiences patients erroneously feel are repeating themselves in the present. As a result, they react inappropriately.

Paleontological psychology is uncovering a patient's past based on the person's behavior in the present, a little bit of information about the patient's past and taking a leap of faith that there is continuity in the person's behavior. The therapist cannot prove the continuity because he has few facts. The therapist then derives a direction that may be incorrect but a good try, based on nothing more than his ideas about that person's past.

Direction in Life as Pathology. A person gets experience by exploring, trying, and being curious. In some people this process stops. Their experience becomes encapsulated because they have a preconceived notion of what they want to do in life. This applies to any person but is particularly pathological in an inexperienced adolescent. If the individual is trying to gain experience to help them arrive at a decision, their behavior is not pathological. Some people make up their minds based on their inability or fear of getting the experience they need.

Focusing on a Symptom

Focus in psychotherapy means concentrating on a symptom as the center of a theory and leaving out its peripheral connections which are the patient's personality. Like many other people, therapists have a tendency, once they get a hold of an idea, to beat it to death. Although practitioners need to remain loose and open to all kinds of ideas, this tendency to fasten onto a concept closes their minds. This natural way of getting comfortable is what therapists have to fight against. In this work, therapists must not marry a symptom to a theory, because this encapsulates them and their patients. Therapists have to continually pick and discard from many ideas about a symptom. They should relax, let come what will, try a theory to see how it works, and if it does not work, use another idea.

Therapists should not call their patients' attention to symptoms too quickly. It stops persons from expressing their feelings with the vigor and lack of inhibition that gives therapists an idea of that with which they are dealing.

The three factors to consider in focusing on a symptom are:

1. How the patient is affected by the symptom. What does it do to the way she lives?
2. How the therapist is affected by the symptom. Is he able to cope with his reaction to it?
3. Is the therapist interested in the symptom? Does she recognize what is a symptom?

Too narrow a focus creates blockage. Any time patients tell their therapists what they want to work on, they get blocked; they quickly run out of things to say. For example, a patient states she wants to work on her relationship with men. The therapist starts by explaining right away her relationship with men is not localized in the way pain is in a medical problem.

The therapist has to work on the patient's whole point of view— her relationships with men, women, and children. She must let the therapist know what happens in any relationship so they can uncover the underlying pattern. Even though relationships with men are a problem for her, she cannot concentrate on this alone and expect a change.

NOTE

1. J. P. Chaplin, *Dictionary of Psychology*, revised ed., Laurel Editions (New York: Dell, 1984), p. 209.

2

The Preparation for Psychotherapy

CHARACTER ARMOR

Character

In this chapter, I begin by contrasting how Wilhelm Reich explains character in *Character Analysis* and how I understand character.[1] I use his concept of character armor but see character differently.

Character as Seen by Reich

Reich has stated,

Certain clinical experiences make it necessary to distinguish among various resistances we meet, a certain group as *character resistances*. They get their specific stamp not from their content but from the patient's specific way of acting and reacting. The compulsive character develops specifically different resistances than does the hysterical character; the latter different resistances from the impulsive or neurasthenic character. The *form* of the typical reactions which differ from character to character—though the content may be the same—*is determined by the infantile experiences just like the content of the symptoms or phantasies.*[2]

Reich also has written,

While the symptom corresponds essentially to a single experience or striving, the character represents the specific way of being an individual, an expression of his total past. For this reason a symptom may develop suddenly while each individual character trait takes years to develop.[3]

Reich appears to see the expression of character determined by the diagnostic category. There are only as many characters as there are categories. The emphasis in both these statements is that character is developed by experience and, therefore, implies it is changed by further experiences.

Reich wrote, "During analysis the character of a patient soon becomes a resistance. That is, in ordinary life, the character plays the same role as in analysis: that of a psychic protection mechanism. The individual is 'characterologically armored' against the outer world and his inner drives."[4] Here character acts as an overlay to protect the individual's self. Character, as a defense mechanism, is different from the kind of person a human being is. By this view, people who present themselves as rough and tough characters could really be very gentle people who never dare show it.

As I See Character

Character is the manner and means people use to express their need for fulfillment. Character is what the self—conscious and unconscious—does and how it does it. I discuss the self in Chapter 5. What people want and the way they set about getting what they want reveals their character. If they want to get rid of something because they feel it is going to destroy them, that also defines their characters. These two wants work together: while wanting to get rid of something, people think about what they want in its place, something more in keeping with their character. The more that needs and self are one, the more animal a character is. Some distance between needs and self humanizes character. People totally absorbed in satisfying a need are not themselves, nor are they aware of themselves. They are instruments for achieving an end. This is seen in animals who tend to be completely absorbed in whatever they are doing.

Character is the result of genetic endowment. Although the

specific genes that make up a character cannot be pinpointed, a certain kind of behavior runs in families, irrespective of how family members are reared. Newborn babies in a hospital nursery behave in ways that are recognized by the nurses as characteristic for only that baby. Therefore, character does not change. The self adapts by learning to use other resources to meet its need for fulfillment in its own characteristic way.

When therapists apply this concept of character to all their patients, it does two important things: One, it helps therapists to know their limits. Two, it indicates how therapists can help patients within this limitation. Take, for example, a woman who was born with strong masculine tendencies. After growing up as a tomboy, this woman lived for years with her proneness to male behavior; trying to be a woman, she failed and was frustrated by the failure. Her therapist told her, "This is the way you are. Your basic masculine inclinations cannot be removed. You must become aware of your masculine tendencies so that you can know when they are detrimental and when they work for you." By not trying to make her more feminine, the therapist dealt with what is.

To the extent that patients are fearful, they are also rigid. Their rigidity is a facade of inflexible behavior so people cannot see what they are like. The therapist sees what the patient is hiding by understanding what is uncharacteristic for that patient. Uncharacteristic means detouring the expression of feelings and emotions natural to the person because of fear. This detour is not directly reacting to a situation; instead, the emotions and feelings belonging to that experience show up somewhere else at another time.

People require so many facades to fit into situations that behavior can be defined as the manipulation of facades as a means of survival. The ability to manipulate facades is the means of survival, however, not the facades themselves. Any situation allows for a variety of acceptable facades. Character is how a person uses the available facades to fit into a situation to meet the self's needs. A facade that hides character is a form of uncharacteristic behavior and, as such, is character armor. Rigidity, referred to in the previous paragraph, is an example of this.

Summary

Reich sees character as a defense mechanism whether used as armor or not. I see it as the direct, natural expression of the self. Fear motivates a person's use of character as a defense mechanism; this is uncharacteristic behavior.

Reich sees character as an expression of the patient's total past, created by experience and changed by experience. I see character as genetically determined and not changeable.

Reich sees as many characters as there are diagnostic categories. I say there are as many different characters as there are human beings.

Character Armor

Reich and I agree that character armor is how persons use their characters as forms of resistance. Resistance is the way people react to inner and outer stimuli so that they are not overwhelmed by their emotions and feelings.

Character armor is ego-syntonic behavior. Such persons feel that pathology, which is not natural to them, is their natural way of behaving. Ego-syntonic pathology is like a foreign body that has become so much a part of the persons that they are not aware of it. Other people are aware of the abnormality. Yet, these persons are able to rationalize, convince themselves, and try to convince other people that there's nothing wrong with them.

Character armor interferes with and stops treatment. It keeps self-awareness intellectual by not letting patients feel what they know. Only when people feel what they understand can change occur. The armor can form such a strong resistance that no progress is made and treatment comes to a halt. In the beginning of treatment, the emphasis is on eroding character armor.

Eroding Character Armor

In dealing with character armor, the term I continually use is some form of the word *erode*. This is done deliberately. The most damaging thing a therapist can do is to remove a person's character armor prematurely. Having no other way to live, the patient is overwhelmed by anxiety and becomes psychotic. It is as if the therapist tossed the person naked into a freezing blizzard. Therapists remove character armor very gradually to prevent patient breakdown. Even under the most controlled circumstances, a therapist can only guess whether he is eroding too fast and may wind up with a prepsychotic patient on his hands. The reduction of character armor always increases anxiety because patients have to learn new ways to survive. During this time they need the help and support of their therapists to hold themselves together.

The general approach is to try to erode patients' character armor by making them aware of what they are doing. Therapists begin by making them aware intellectually of what they cannot tolerate emotionally. With hostile patients, therapists can demonstrate how the patients behave: "Here's the way you look. Here's what you do. I want to point it out to you. It's important that we explore and understand it. Unless you help do this we're not going to get anywhere. I'm not asking you to stop doing it. I'm asking you to listen to me, to see what I'm trying to help you see. That's all." Therapists should keep doing this until the hostile behavior stops, which will eventually happen.

As character armor is eroded, patients go from the intellectual to emotional level, where they feel what they know. When patients first see therapists, they talk intellectually about their thoughts and ideas. Those thoughts and ideas have their basis in patients' emotions and feelings and are like the foam on a glass of beer. When therapists scrape off the foam, patients have nothing left to say except to begin to share what they really feel.

Character armor is nothing but a facade patients have used effectively for years. The facade is the way patients present themselves to the world. Although patients believe the presentation is the way they are, that is mostly false. Therapists start patients questioning and disbelieving what they think they are. When character armor is reduced, no matter how therapists do it, the rest happens by itself: The persons under the character armor come to the fore.

Psychology as a Religion. Many people in psychotherapy come from an environment where psychology is almost as important to their lives as manure is to plants. Psychology becomes a kind of religion. Most people do not have a framework to their life.

They have no center. Psychology and therapy are made that center. For treatment purposes, this is bad because it leads to much intellectualizing about emotions and feelings instead of experiencing them. The erosion of character armor destroys this facade against feeling.

THE EROSION OF CHARACTER ARMOR

Preparation

Preparing for Treatment

Therapists are always triggering emotions in patients, for there is no other way of doing treatment. Many practitioners think that getting emotions out into the open is all that is necessary for effective treatment. The problem is not only getting the emotions out but also deciding what the therapist and patient are to do with them. Preparation is getting patients ready to do their part in treatment.

Talking about emotions and feelings is nonsense to anybody not prepared to listen. When therapists talk about emotions, they trigger a desire in their patients to escape. They make these people feel miserable because all their lives patients have worked to repress emotions so as not to face them. Now by talking about them the therapist makes these persons feel great pain and fear. Practitioners should not start by arousing fears in patients so that they have to run away from treatment. Therapists must put what they have to say in an intellectual context which people can understand and think about. If patients think long enough, they become bewildered. Their emotional problems trigger a number of reactions to what their therapists say that makes their thinking confused. Then they can call on their therapists for help with their feelings, which they could not do before.

Patients should know their therapists are preparing them for treatment. They should get an idea about what they and their therapists are trying to do, what the patient's part is and what the therapist's part is. Therapists should explain and explain and explain so that patients can understand and help therapists do what both want to do. The explanation is an elastic outline, the format within which therapists and patients work together in preparation for what is to happen. It must merge into participation. Having an idea of what can and cannot happen gives patients a sense of security and helps to prevent psychosis. Every time patients omit doing their part, therapists cannot do their part. Patients sabotage treatment when they neglect what they are supposed to do or do what they should not do.

Therapists note what their patients do in a session, point out to them what happened, and briefly tie the observation back to what they are trying to do. This is done over and over and never stops. Therapists use whatever their patients do in the interview to prepare them for treatment. Therapists keep their patients looking at themselves and questioning themselves as they try to erode the patient's character armor.

When persons are aware of their feelings, therapists have to help them find a way to think and talk about these emotions. In that way, therapists are reducing the possibility of emotionally inundating their patients and having them become psychotic. Patients do not feel they are going to lose control over themselves because they understand what is happening. Despite going through all kinds of anguish, they assign their meaning to their pain in terms of their feelings and eventually their thinking. Patients are in treatment to arrive at their own interpretation of their lives as therapists help them to gradually increase their awareness of themselves and their behavior.

Patients have to believe that what they and their therapists are doing has a cumulative effect. Cumulative means nothing may happen today, tomorrow, or the next day, but on the fourth day something is going to happen that takes in all the previous days. When patients feel that, therapists do not have to work under the pressure of making something therapeutic happen every session. Therapists explain that as a good cup of coffee needs to percolate, so does much therapeutic work.

This approach gets through to the rigid people the professional literature says cannot be reached, especially those with character disorders. Therapists appeal to what they consider their strongest point: their intellect. Once the practitioner has explained long enough for the patients to understand, the patient begins to try doing what is asked. If they cannot do it, therapists get some insight into the nature of their patients' resistance and figure out what to do instead.

After the opening few minutes of each session, every person in treatment tends to forget what the therapist says. All the different forms of preparation are continually repeated to counteract this amnesia. The preparation can be decreased when the patient becomes a little bit involved. For instance, when words trigger memories suffused with emotion of past experiences, they pull up chains of associations with emotions and feelings attached to them.

Even though the patient does many of the things asked of her, the therapist should not assume that preparation can be discontinued. The practitioner will find that the patient has forgotten other aspects of preparation. It goes on till the day the therapist discharges the patient. At that time, the therapist is preparing the patient to distinguish between pathological problems and life problems, that with which she needs help and that with which she should help herself.

Other Reasons for Preparation

To Avoid Acting Out. Once therapists have provided patients with the necessary words and ideas to talk about their emotions and feelings, the possibility of the patients acting out is reduced. Acting out is the compulsive expression of feelings through doing something because talking is not possible. A person acting out is like a child who wants his mother's attention but does not know how to get it except by tugging at her clothing. Patients have to be taught they are acting out their feelings and then helped to talk about them instead of doing something. The more they are able to put feelings into words and talk about them, the less the need to do something and the more control they have over themselves. What blood is to the physical system, words are to the psychic. Words are the blood of the psyche.

To Reduce Resistance. Without an intellectual context in which to think about feelings, patients' resistance is strengthened because they are unable to understand their feelings. Resistance is a fearful reaction to uncovering emotions and feelings. Patients have difficulty discriminating between feelings they can cope with and those that, for them, are dangerous. Therefore, feelings carry the potential for overwhelming patients. The only way to cope in that situation is not to permit awareness of most feelings to occur. There is no intrinsic relationship between intelligence and the understanding of the unconscious. The therapist has to provide the words and ideas.

To Teach Patients. Therapists organize their thinking about a patient around certain principles or theories they have learned or used. The patients organize what therapists say not so much on principle but on what has the greatest meaning to them. Therapists have to teach patients to use the concepts they are applying.

People are used to coping with experiences individually. They count each marble of experience separately, one, two, three, four, overlooking how they are connected. They get used to counting those marbles and just go on that way. Patients are not in therapy to learn to count marbles better. Therapists have to help people deal with concepts that are more important than the counting. Why do patients need to count marbles? Are they afraid somebody will steal them or that they do not know how to count? Factual detail is not as important as the emotions and feelings motivating patients' behavior. Therapists have to help persons find concepts into which the emotions and feelings can be placed so they can begin to think about them.

Practitioners reach patients through the way they think and what they think of themselves. People think in certain ways based on their work, education, and life experiences. For example, if a person presents himself as a scientist, the therapist's question is, "How does a scientist think?" The answer is that a scientist believes he has solved an emotional problem when he has thought about it scientifically. Actually, he has just looked at it in a certain way. When the therapist gets the scientist/patient to see this, he becomes confused. He asks, "Look, where do we go from here?" Then the therapist can start the preparation for treatment.

To Keep Expectations Realistic. When people come for the first few times and the crisis has not subsided, they are very emotional and tell their therapists many things. By the time they come the sixth or seventh time, the pressure to reveal themselves has petered out and they claim, "Well, I've told you everything." Patients believe that therapy is a talking cure. After they have talked so emotionally they feel there's nothing else to talk about; now their therapists should set about curing them. If therapists prepare patients for what is supposed to happen, then expectations of a cure do not occur. Patients have to accept their therapists' explanation that other emotions are as important as those they have expressed; these have not been uncovered and contribute to the problem.

Introducing Interventions

Another form of preparation is to introduce patients to the interventions. An intervention is a way of finding out what patients are feeling. They need to understand they are practicing using the interventions—that this is not yet therapy but the preparation for it. As they begin learning, practical results emerge. They know how they feel, which tells them what they want, which gives them an idea of what they want to do. A conflict means there are additional feelings in the situation that need to be discovered.

In the beginning of treatment, the emphasis is not on the content of what the interventions uncover but on patients' ability to do them. The interventions are quite simple. The patients' inability to participate in an intervention usually is a form of resistance. As the resistances begin to emerge they highlight patients' problems. For example, patients who cry and are unable to put what they are feeling into words or pictures may indicate persons who cannot let themselves know what they are feeling. Patients' understanding of how the interventions uncover resistances help them to have the necessary patience to endure this stage of treatment.

Concurrently, therapists are trying to help them cope with the problems in their lives. This gives therapists reasons for using interventions. If practitioners can determine what patients are feeling, possibly they can make connections with their problems. In the beginning of treatment, the major emphasis is on the intervention of integration which I discuss in Chapter 4.

The Need for Crisis

A crisis represents an emotional accumulation seeking to explode. This explosion dissipates the accumulation. Even so, the accumulation is just temporarily disposed of; it will build up again. Therefore, a crisis is pregnant with possibilities for treatment because all kinds of emotions and feelings are more available to work with.

In many instances, therapy is effective only when a person is drowning in the middle of the ocean and the therapist is her life raft. On that basis, therapy often continues; if, however, the therapist is not a life raft, it stops. The therapist creates a crisis by increasing the patient's anxiety when the situation is temporarily stabilized and the person does not see the importance of continuing. Preparation helps therapists to hold the crisis they have created in an intellectual context which keeps the patient from being overwhelmed.

The Intellectual Approach

Coping with Emotions Intellectually

The intellectual approach is based on the fact that ideas can trigger emotions. An example of this is the patient who was afraid to marry his girlfriend because he had already been through one bad marriage. My comment that he was behaving protectively, as a husband would, produced grimaces of distaste and shudders of revulsion. He thought about his reactions and realized he did not want to know he felt protective toward her.

In this instance, an idea about his behavior triggered the patient's feelings; like water poured into a container, they were given the intellectual category of "behaving protectively, like a husband." Now he could think about his behavior and begin to let himself feel what he was doing. He could use his intellect, along with his emotions, to think further about the situation. He began to understand his behavior and gained greater comprehension of his fears. The intellectual approach counteracted his—and most patients'—tendency to depend too much on the therapist. It supports the desire of people to be on their own.

The more common approach uses emotions to trigger emotions. A patient tells the therapist about a traumatic experience. The therapist says, "Tell me more about it. Tell me more." As the patient continues, there is a series of internal emotional explosions, like a string of firecrackers, because the retelling of the experience reactivates the feelings that accompanied it. Once the therapist starts one firecracker, all the others go off. The usual approach gets emotions out but cannot control the rate of release so that the patient is not overwhelmed by them.

Using ideas to trigger reactions keeps emotions from getting out of control because they are contained within the intellectual framework created for them. If patients become inundated, therapists simply stop introducing ideas that trigger emotions. The main purpose is to protect patients and therapists from uncontrolled emotional reactions to treatment ending in psychosis. Therapists must be aware of the consequences that could occur as a result of what they are doing. Therapeutic success is not as important as the understanding behind it.

In an intellectual approach, patients look at feelings objectively. Feelings are not exaggerated by patients or therapists, as happens when therapists keep asking their patients, "How do you feel?" Then patients begin to exaggerate their feelings to make an impression on their therapists. An intellectual approach keeps the exaggeration to a minimum.

Free association tends to inundate patients in emotion because so much gets triggered. Their emotions overwhelm their intellects. Intellectual categories are needed to help avoid a psychotic break. When individuals use their intellects to cope with emotion, they are in charge.

Therapists can do quite a lot if they concentrate on knowing how to use ideas effectively, rather than using free association. It does not matter how concrete or unintellectual people are; they become very smart when it comes to survival. The therapist's function is to reach people through ideas that trigger their emotions and feelings; that is how psychotherapy becomes effective.

Avoiding the Unconscious

Wilhelm Reich sees the erosion of character armor as preparation for psychoanalysis where the intent is to uncover as much of the unconscious as possible. Practitioners using an intellectual approach erode character armor only to the extent needed to get at what the patients are feeling. Where possible, every effort is made to work with the conscious self. They resort to the unconscious only when necessary and then for no longer than needed. Many therapists look at emotional problems as reactions that have become emotionally congealed. Patients are unable to directly express themselves. Focusing on the emotions involved and their relation to each other, therapists tend to ignore their connection to an outer reality. Such practitioners may interpretively say, "You are too anxious because you accepted your father's denigrations and feel you can't cope adequately with the current situation." Then the therapists converge on the feelings of inadequacy or anxiety.

The intellectual approach starts with the assumption that all emotional problems are attached to something concrete. A congealed emotional problem is a group of responses to an intricate concrete situation in which the unexpressed emotions have gone off in all directions. For example, a youngster of two or three may have tantrums; the child is frustrated because he is not old enough to do what he wants to do. It is very simple, but not to the youngster who raises holy hell. The child does not understand that he is trying to live beyond his limits. He is not mature enough to do what he is attempting, and the frustration trigger the tantrum.

Persons with severe emotional problems are in a similar situation. They have tried to do certain things over and over again and botched them. Failure triggers strong feelings, even anger against themselves. Their therapists' concern is what to do about this.

These emotional problems can be dealt with on two levels. One is on the surface: Therapists find out what concrete frustrations their patients are experiencing and try to help them to solve the puzzle. Maybe the patients cannot do it or have not done it correctly because they do not have the skill. Getting an understanding of why they cannot do it, patients try a different way. Up to this time, they have lost hope and feel they are no good. This is different from encapsulating a problem, which occurs when a psychological interpretation is imposed on a patient's behavior.

At the second level, therapists explore an emotional problem in terms of the concrete situation, discuss it, and bring out the feelings that are there: one, two, three, four, five, six. Patients then put their own interpretation on them. They do not encapsulate themselves because as they try to untangle their feelings about the concrete situation they will, in the process, react emotionally to what they find out and become free to try to resolve the emotional problem again. Encapsulating makes patients' feelings unknown to them, thus leaving them with no idea of what to do.

Therapists should not support patients who just vent their feelings. Instead, as they bring in concrete situations for consideration, practitioners should explore them and serve as mirrors by saying, "Well, from what you're telling me, this is what I see. Is this the way it is?" Then the patient corrects the therapist as necessary. Between them they untangle the situation so that the patient can understand what is happening.

The Intellectual Approach vs. Theorizing or Interpretation

An interpretation or theory, which is also intellectual, takes a mass of material and conceptualizes it in relation to the patient's conduct and feelings. The intellectual approach concentrates on a small segment of the patient's behavior and connects it closely to what the person is feeling. If the therapist interjects a theory or interpretation, she waters down the impact of the intellectual approach because in a large body of material the connections to a feeling are not as immediate.

Creating Distance

One of the things that makes therapists effective is that often they are able to see not only the obvious but also that which does not meet the eye. This makes their patients respond, "I never thought of that." The fact that their patients never thought of it until now gives patients distance from their emotions. Even though their problems may remain, patients are able to see their problems and rise above them.

As people start treatment, they are dominated by their problems, upset by them. Within the first 10 or 12 interviews, the intellectual approach should have increased the patients' awareness of themselves and others. As they gain an awareness of how they are affected, they are able to step back and look at their problems. This is a gain in that the patient's self has separated from the problem.

In Lieu of Cure

There is no end to psychotherapy, only intervals when patients do not see their therapists. Persons who have proven susceptible to life's strains need therapists as their insurance against the inclemencies of existence. When patients get into trouble and do not know what to do, they see their therapists again and their upsets subside. The problem is that patient and professional both insist there is a "cure." It is hard to dislodge that attitude. Other than the medical concept of lesion removal, I do not have a clear idea of what is meant by cure or no cure.

Somehow what people understand intellectually can affect them emotionally. When the problem situation presents itself again, they avoid it out of an understanding that otherwise they will get into trouble. There is an emotional charge in the trouble that they were not aware of before but they are now. They know what happens if they do not protect themselves. Internal reactions warn them to "Watch out!" They feel pain; intellectually they wonder, "Who needs this?" Eventually, on an emotional level, persons feel "I don't want to get hurt."

In the intellectual approach, the attempt is to try to make patients intellectually aware of the emotional problems they have and the impossibility of curing them. If patients want to live happier lives, they have to control their destructive tendencies by volition. Regarding volition, I only want to go to the very outer edge of this metaphysical subject. In the context of this discussion, will is the self-preserving instinct becoming aware of an objective as a means of saving the person. By arousing patients' self-preserving instincts, therapists enable them to achieve some control over their self-destructive tendencies.

We know—but cannot prove—that there is an instinct for self-preservation. The need, the urge to live, is there. When therapists make them aware their lives are threatened, patients try to continue living by finding some way of defending against the threat. Therapists can use this instinct very purposefully, but they have to know what they are doing because they can get into a lot of trouble.

Substituting an Idea for an Experience. Human life is constantly aware of its own survival because human beings can anticipate their dying. If people can have the idea of their death, they can also think of their survival. Therapists have to trigger an idea of death, which in turn triggers the idea of survival, which in turn triggers the idea of protection. More simply the idea is, "You're going to kill yourself," "You're going to get killed," or "You are involved in a slow process of suicide." Human beings cannot experience something before they experience it. So while therapists cannot trigger the actual situation, they can trigger the idea of the occurrence. This triggers the feelings that go with that state. In this way, therapists expose their patients to experiences which they learn from on an emotional level. Truly, this limited exposure lacks the ramifications and impact of reality but it is enough to galvanize patients into thinking about how to protect themselves.

Ideas Should Not Be Ends

Therapists must distinguish between ideas and emotional reactions to them. Ideas are words and words are the only way to verbally express an emotion. Ideas themselves are unimportant. The emotions triggering ideas or the ideas triggering emotions are important. The idea and the emotion are different; an idea may trigger an entirely unrelated emotion.

For example, imagine a table between us. What would happen if I used this table to remind you of the tables in your home when you were 12 years old? When this table, in the present, becomes a past table in your home all the positive and negative emotions attached to that idea come to the fore. Your parents and you ate at this table. How did that feel? It could bring up so much if it is like a table in your home but all those associations are lost when the interest in the table is only as an idea here and now in the present.

Awareness

Therapeutic awareness is a formulation in the therapist's mind to catch impressions of which the patient is unaware. It is an ability to organize data the therapist did not have before becoming aware. It is a sieve with big holes which awareness has made smaller. Now the therapist can recognize the significant facts and emotions that otherwise would have gone by him.

Self-Awareness Erodes Character Armor

Most people do not know how others react to them. In emotionally disturbed persons, this tendency not to know or to definitely not want to know how they look to others is stronger than ordinary. Many times these people can barely look at themselves in mirrors because they do not want to know how dissatisfied they are with what they see. The purpose of self-awareness is to have the person become aware there is a difference between what they think they are and what their emotional reactions say they are.

Awareness Triggers Emotion. If we stop and think of what emotion does, we see that it is explosive. Patients who can watch their own explosiveness as their therapists do, from the outside, develop a little awareness of themselves. This awareness triggers emotions because it affects individuals' self-images and they become ashamed of themselves. It is the failure of themselves to themselves; that is, "I should be different and I'm trying to be different, but I really cannot, as yet, come up to what I think I should be."

Awareness in therapy is painful because whatever people discover about themselves is done intellectually but they have to find a place for it emotionally. Awareness has to displace an existing emotional arrangement within patients, and that displacement is very painful. Each time the same discovery is made, people have to displace less and less until there is a place established for whatever they have become aware of: it fits in.

Avoid Why. When therapists point out to their patients what they are doing, they should not ask why. Once patients have a reason, they have a way to escape from their behavior by losing themselves in speculations. They rationalize rather than trying for emotional changes that could modify their behavior. Therapists should keep pointing out what patients are doing. Although they cannot do this too often, they should not tell patients why. In the beginning of treatment, the reason is tied up with so many other aspects of patients that therapists cannot discuss them all. It takes in too much of the patients' whole personalities.

The reason goes to a level neither therapists nor patients are ready for until patients have a great awareness of what they are supposed to do and how they are to do it. Until then, the "why" is an intellectual discussion without any emotional modification.

Emotional Dimensions Erode Character Armor

Patients reveal emotional dimensions by going back to the same subject, experience, or symptom again and again. Each repetition brings out new dimensions of the material. Additional emotions and feelings are discovered, or forgotten parts return, or the matter is viewed from a different emotional context. The therapist's job is to demonstrate to the patient that each repetition is not an exact duplication of what was said before. There is always some new aspect to the material. It is a way of uncovering as much as was significant in an experience.

Because words trigger emotions, the therapist's most important tool is language. Of necessity, language takes on new meanings with new experiences. When the patient talked about an experience a number of months ago, it had different connotations than it does now. Something is added or subtracted or the emphasis is different or the context in which the subject is raised has changed. There is always something new. The nature of language is to both exclude and include emotions, depending on how it is used. Language controls emotions and feelings and how they are expressed through concepts. It is not only how people talk or what they talk about but also where and when they talk and with whom they talk and what the talking means. People talk about their work differently when they are on the job than when they are at home.

Application

Symptoms appear in disguise in various contexts at different times. The therapist learns which symptoms repeat themselves at different times and under what conditions. Let us say the patient distrusts men. At different times in various contexts this suspicion is expressed. However, the suspicion can be so disguised by its context that it will not look like suspicion. The therapist's job is to watch for a selected symptom. Only as it comes in different contexts and the therapist points it out does the effect on the patient become cumulative. The therapist should hook these examples of pathological behavior together.

A patient of mine brought up the same questions again and again: "Does my wife love me for me or for what I can give her? She left her last job slyly, never letting the boss know what she was doing until she already had the next job. Will she leave me the same way, so that it will be too late for me to do anything about it?" He felt that no one did things as well as he so that if he asked someone to do something either it would not be done on time or done right. He tended to overreact to his employees' behavior, berating them unnecessarily. He usually put negative meanings on his experiences. When these symptoms were pointed out to him again and again, he could accept them as different forms of a pervasive underlying anxiety. He began to question what he was afraid of.

The other way to use emotional dimensions is to let patients talk about the same experience again and again until they have uncovered the emotions and feelings that brought on the situation. One patient constantly complained he had been cruelly abandoned by his last girlfriend after she had badly used him. The therapist encouraged him to talk about what had happened in the relationship. Slowly, as he repeated certain incidents again and again, the patient became aware he had simply wanted to go to bed with the woman and did not care for her very much at all. She had left him after she became aware he had little affection for her.

Transition from the Emotional to the Intellectual

When therapists first meet with patients, they usually start on an emotional level because the patient is emotionally upset. Neither knows what the problem is, what is to be done, or if the patient can be helped. Gradually the emphasis should become more evenly balanced between the emotional and intellectual levels. The intellectual level should lead to the question of a practical goal or goals and how to attain them.

Therapists have to deal with some problems emotionally because they come to them that way. Until therapists take care of those issues they cannot do anything else. Therapists bring in the intellect as a balance against emotion when pleasure seeking becomes destructive to the self and other people. Intellectual ideas condition the emotions and to some extent determine which ones arise. The meaning we give to the situation determines how we feel about it and triggers other feelings in association with it. This is how emotional reactions are changed.

The transition to the intellectual level comes when:

1. The crisis is reduced.
2. The patient has some idea of how she and the therapist are going to work.
3. The patient has some ability to look inside herself and report what she finds, such as dreams or fantasies.

In the beginning, the therapist should shift from an intellectual to an emotional approach (1) when he needs to counteract the patient's intellectuality, or (2) to supplement the therapist's knowledge of a person, adding to what was already arrived at by the intellectual approach.

Therapists should consider a case as probably having two parts, with a relationship between those parts. Part one is the emotional factor manifested by the patient's presentation of her situation at the beginning of therapy. Part two is the intellectual factor which is a collection of categories developed for receiving emotions. The emotion goes into an intellectual category expressly designed for it. Both parts should be applied to the problem itself so that the problem is resolved or reduced. Life always creates new problems. The patient copes with most of them based on what the categories of the intellectual approach taught her. If she gets stuck, she can return to the therapist for help.

Implementing the Intellectual Approach— Conceptualization

General Explanation

Concept: 1. a general idea or meaning usually mediated by a word, symbol, or sign. 2. an idea which combines several elements from different sources into a single notion. The concept *mammal* refers to a variety of divergent species all of which have several attributes in common. Concepts are formed by a process of abstraction, which is then followed by a process of generalization. A child, for example, abstracts the concept of roundness from his limited experiences with balls, oranges and the moon. He then learns to generalize the concept to all objects having the same characteristic shape. Abstract concepts are concepts such as number, goodness, or quality, which cannot be attributed to a specific object or events. Concrete concepts refer to a particular instance or object, as opposed to a general instance or quality of many objects.[5]

An abstraction is an idea about ideas. For example, I may equate roundness with good and squareness with evil. Most people live in abstraction. By the way they live, they exemplify the abstraction. A patient's problem is a distortion of an abstraction. She has a distorted view about certain ideas. The first step is to get her into a framework I call conceptualization.

Conceptualizing the problem locates the distorted idea or itch that makes scratching necessary. Organizing the patient's emotions highlights the idea that does not belong there. Locating it does not stop the itching, but at least the therapist and patient know where it is and can try to correct the distortion. Conceptualization deals with pieces and parts of human behavior. It does not develop a single theory covering all aspects of a person's behavior.

Conceptualizations are intellectual gimmicks for which emotions have very little respect. When they want to break out and if emotions are strong enough, they push intellectual gimmicks aside. All this leads to a platitude that relationships and the way people live alone or together depends on emotion not concepts. A woman in love with a man may know she deserves a better man, but she loves that particular man. The love is an emotion; the idea tells her it is wrong to love the man.

Psychological reality is the patient's innermost private life. It is a description of the person's emotional needs and state. For treatment purposes, the most important parts of psychological reality are the distortions responsible for the patient's emotional problems. All people have a limited view of reality. They see only that for which they know they are looking. This seeking is determined by the emotional needs of which they are aware. Their concept of reality is further constricted by the degree of emotional disturbance which prevents them from knowing what their needs are. A psychological reality, with its distortions of the past and the misinterpretations of the present, with its energy-consuming use of fantasy, with its emphasis on escaping from anxiety no matter what the price, with its use of physical symptoms as one of the important outlets for frustration and emotional strangulation, is opposed to the reality represented by psychotherapy and the therapist. The practitioner's aim is to present alternative, clarifying concepts that modify the patient's psychological reality.

Going from Effect to Effect. In this approach the therapist works from effect to effect. She does something which triggers an emotion in the patient. This action I call an intervention. The therapist says, "Look, see how you reacted? See how you're feeling? What does that mean?" The therapist gives no answers. The questions are left in the patient's hands. The effect of the intervention, the patient's reaction, tells the practitioner what is going on inside the patient at that time. From this, the therapist deduces what to do next. Another intervention is tried, and another effect is achieved which either confirms that the therapist understands what is happening or that she needs to rethink what she is doing. Again the patient is asked, "What does that mean?"

The therapist can assume that the patient's reaction to an intervention is either pathological or has many pathological elements in it because the person is emotionally disturbed. The response is on the surface where the both of them can see it. The therapist gets more reactions as time goes on and organizes them so the patient can also look at his responses and get some distance from them. That means the therapist has conceptualized the patient's reactions, not their cause. The therapist is trying to enable the patient to see himself and modify his behavior so that eventually he can deal with the behavior himself.

Therapists have to work from effect to effect because the mind-body problem, the way a thought becomes an emotional and physical reaction or vice versa, remains unsolved. Therefore, therapists use psychological theories based on many human beings and melt them down to fit a particular person. They use theories pragmatically, that is, trying several interventions to determine if the theories fit. For treatment purposes, it is enough to know they fit. This method is nothing but a means of applying various theories pragmatically.

The Reason for Conceptualization. Most people, especially those who are emotionally disturbed and in a state of anxiety, cannot organize their thoughts and put them in categories. In fact they do not think; they react mainly with explosive emotion. What they need is a thought to organize their reactions for them, giving them some idea of what makes their emotions explode all over the place. Such a conceptualization enables them to cope with their emotions because now they fall into understood categories. Once they have the concept, the explosions transform themselves into a main thought that patients can try to develop further.

A patient once told me, "I don't believe I accept your theory."

"Then give me yours," I said. "I'll listen to you."

"I haven't got any."

"Then you have to accept mine until you get yours."

The therapist listens to the other person, giving her the freedom and choice to come up with an alternate concept. But the practitioner has nothing to listen to if she has nothing to tell. Then the patient has to listen to the therapist.

Conceptualization and Intellectualization. When the therapist conceptualizes with a patient, they are creating a framework for what they both believe is or could be the problem. The therapist creates an intellectual picture of the problem to begin with because the patient cannot involve himself emotionally. A conceptualization is a rough sketch that the patient can fill in.

When the therapist intellectualizes, she is talking about ideas, lecturing. The patient receives it all without having to struggle for understanding. The therapist makes the sketch and fills it in. There is nothing for the patient to add.

Conceptualizing a Patient. Therapists work with people as individuals. The practitioner must not forget to look into the context in which the patient lives otherwise he becomes a person minus a mother, father, family, or job. It is like trying to study a live fish out of water.

At the same time, to know a person the therapist must individualize him. Every person is made up of consistent inconsist-encies that distinguish them from everyone else. An example of this was the well-to-do woman who grew up in poverty. In her childhood home the bed sheets were changed rarely and smelled bad. Now she does not care how dirty the rest of the house gets but the sheets have to be clean and fresh-smelling. Bed sheets may have to be changed every other day to satisfy her. Another name for this is a hang-up. A hang-up has embedded in it some of the character of that person. Besides rejecting her upbringing, this patient basically liked to have things clean and in their place. When the therapist gets to know the person, the hang-up is no longer a hang-up. It belongs to that person's behavior, but she feels it does not belong. All this refers to the fact that a person presents a characteristic attitude and behavior to the world in-cluding her hang-ups, her consistent inconsistencies. These have to be included in any conceptualization the therapist makes about the patient as an individual.

Conceptualizing with Adolescents. To experience is to let yourself feel whatever your reactions are and put them into words. The understanding is retrospective in that you must have the expe-rience first to think about what happened afterward. A person at, say, 40 has had a lot of experiences he has not put into words. It is a jumble, but he has something to select, to start with. It is questionable if adolescents can really experience and know what they are experiencing: they not only have to put it into words, but they also have to compare it with previous experiences to see where it is the same and where it is different. Adolescents are just getting experience. How can they compare when they do not have preceding experiences?

The therapist has to conceptualize more of what is going on for adolescents since they cannot do as much of this as adults can. There is the danger of encapsulating adolescents, of pre-venting them from having the experiences they should have before the therapist organizes it. Conceptualization can be thought of as a road map in that what a person learns in one experience can be used in other new experiences. Adolescents have to travel through life but do not yet have a road or road map. The therapist provides the road map.

Using Conceptualization

Applying Concepts Dynamically. The concept of trust illustrates this idea. Trust means, first of all, your own inner security. In other words, you can trust somebody if you trust yourself. You equate trust with security and security means control. If you do not trust yourself, you have no control of yourself. This leaves you feeling insecure. You can trust somebody when you have the feeling that it does not matter if they fool you because you have a hold on yourself. Whatever you lose you can always get back or rearrange your life so it goes on satisfactorily.

When explaining a concept this way to a person, the practitioner shifts the situation to the patient. The person begins to ask, "Well, what is it that I'm afraid of?" By using a concept operationally the therapist opens up the situation for the patient to do what he believes he should do. The therapist should give the patient functional definitions of an idea and see what he does with it.

Equating Ideas with Experience. Therapists do not realize as fully as they should that in the beginning they start with ideas while their patients start with experiences. And never the twain shall meet until therapists feel—not just know about—the experience of their patients and try to put it in categories of ideas that help patients organize their experiences. To do that, therapists have to use their own experiences which are similar to their patients': the therapist's intellectual concepts are available to the patient only when they are concretized by the other person's experience.

Even though patients' experiences may be varied, all the time they feel alone with them. In some way which cannot be anticipated because it is so different in every situation, the principle is to have patients feel they are not alone, that their experience—not matter how different—is an experience shared by other people. It can be understood. The principle is used from the beginning of treatment until such time as the therapists' ideas become experiences for their patients. Once patients feel they are not alone, they can begin to look at themselves and help their therapists. It is like helping a child get over the fear of a dark room by going into the room with him.

Bringing up the Concept Each Session. I asked one of my patients questions and he put together the solicited information. I said to him, "When we meet again you will have forgotten the concept you put together from the information my questions elicited. We have to do something about this forgetting. We have to bring up this concept again and again."

Either the patient or the therapist brings up the idea each session. The patient may do it because the concept has made him very uncomfortable. He knows the way to decrease his discomfort is by continuing to consider the idea. This helps him to emotionally accept what he arrived at intellectually.

Repetition is for therapists what the drill is for dentists, a tool for cleaning out pathology. There are always two opposite forces in a human being: One makes the person fight treatment every step of the way and not get well. The other makes her try very hard to get well. Call one force self-destruction and the other self-preservation. The therapist is trying to strengthen self-preservation to counter the self-destructive forces. Generally, the patient gets more pleasure out of emotional pathology than being well. The therapist must call to the patient's attention and conceptualize that she is having a good time being self-destructive as against the practitioner's trying to enable her to be more constructive and creative. The therapist should also point out that the patient will not remember this concept the next time or the time after that because her tendency toward self-destruction is very strong and she needs to forget. However, the therapist reminds the patient each time in the hope that she can get at the roots of this self-destruction. The therapist points out the patient's forgetting of the conceptualization is self-destructive to see if the patient's self-preservation can be mobilized.

Ideas Trigger Emotions. When therapists read a book and want to assimilate its ideas into their therapeutic approaches, they have to ask "How would I use them?" The therapist can do one of two things: They can directly apply the ideas to the patient in the form of theories or ask the patient questions in terms of the concepts. In any event, the idea must be clear in the therapist's mind. If the therapist uses confused ideas, he really does not know what they do or where to use them.

Therapists should not take an idea and just try to talk about it; that does not work. To transform an idea into an emotion, the therapist looks for an opportunity to present the idea and talk about it in a general abstract way, emphasizing its positive aspects. The therapist then waits to see how the patient reacts to it. The person may ask questions. This gives the therapist the first hint that the idea is doing something to the patient.

The therapist perseveres with an idea when he is trying to trigger an emotion with it. He keeps banging, banging, banging until the person gets angry and reacts with "That's enough!" That gives the therapist an indication he may have triggered something.

The therapist uses ideas to stimulate other ideas that have painful associations for the patient. This makes the person run away from treatment. If the therapist is able to have the patient understand the importance of triggering these particular painful emotions, she may stay with therapy.

The Results of Conceptualization

1. The intellectual context in which the patient can think and understand himself is created.

2. Acting out is avoided. The conceptualization has given the patient the words and ideas she needs so she could talk about how she feels instead of compulsively doing something about the emotion.

3. Conceptualization leads to the main theme and subthemes in the person's life, of which knowledge is needed to do effective therapy. It also leads to the theories or parts of theories that will fit a particular patient. I discuss theme and theory in Chapter 5.

4. Using the concepts the therapist has given him, the patient develops his own meaning of his behavior.

THE END RESULT OF PREPARATION

Every person, to some extent, is encased in character armor. Before treatment can begin, the character armor has to be sufficiently reduced so that both therapist and patient can find out what the person is feeling. The usual way is to constantly interpret to the patient that her behavior in the interview is a form of resistance. Many patients cannot tolerate this kind of response and discontinue treatment.

A different approach is to try to get through to the patient intellectually because this is the area of his greatest strength, where he feels most safe and comfortable. The first step is preparing the patient for treatment by:

1. Explaining what he and the therapist are going to do and the job each one will have.
2. Giving the patients the words and ideas she needs so she can talk about her emotions and feelings.
3. Introducing the patient to the interventions so he can become familiar with them and adept at using them.
4. Maintaining enough anxiety in the patient so she continues in treatment.

The next step is not to try to uncover feelings but to introduce ideas that can trigger emotions in the patient and then discuss what happens. The intellectual approach deals with small segments of the patient's behavior. The unconscious is avoided when possible. This keeps the patient from being overwhelmed by her emotions and feelings. The therapist must recognize whether an emotional or intellectual approach is necessary. The practitioner uses his awareness of the patient to organize the reactions to ideas into concepts about the person.

Conceptualization is the further implementation of the intellectual approach. It individualizes people and their behavior and feelings. The concepts are dynamic descriptions of the patient's life experience. A person is not the static concept of suffering from free-floating anxiety. Instead, he is climbing high on a ladder he is sure will disappear from underneath him at any time. The concepts are referred back to in each treatment session. Repetition is the tool the therapist uses to clean out pathology. As self-awareness increases, the person realizes there is a difference between the picture he has of himself and what his emotions say he really is. He is now ready to begin exploring what is going on emotionally within him.

All of this goes on at the same time in the beginning. Sometimes one part is emphasized in one session over others but all of these aspects need to be covered to erode character armor.

Warning

If the therapist is effective, some dangerous situations can develop, such as depression, psychotic break, or the person wanting to lose herself in a psychosis. Many times this is unavoidable because the therapist cannot measure how fast the erosion occurred. The character armor is eroded before the patient is ready to cope and live with her awareness of herself. She can no longer repress emotions and feelings and avoid dealing with them. Much anxiety and guilt must be reduced and put back where they belong, as many times they become displaced and distorted. The patient must feel she can depend on the therapist and live out the hymn that goes, "Rock of ages, cleft to me. Let me hide myself in thee."

The Results

1. The possibility of a psychosis is greatly lessened. Words and ideas trigger emotions and feelings at a pace the patient can tolerate. The awareness of emotions triggers further emotional reactions. A short self-sustaining chain of awareness develops, beginning on the intellectual and going to the emotional level. The process can be stopped by not introducing any more ideas that trigger emotions and feelings.

2. The patient's ideas of who and what he is and his way of thinking becomes so confused he is ready to turn to the therapist and ask what to do therapeutically to clarify the situation. He becomes involved in treatment.

3. The patient's resistance to treatment is reduced.

4. The patient participates in the treatment by trying to do the interventions. More is learned about the patient's problem from the difficulties the person encounters in doing what is asked.

5. A much tighter fitting explanation of the patient's behavior and emotions is provided by the intellectual approach.

6. The patient begins to distinguish between the pathology

she needs help with and the life problems that she can cope with by herself.

7. A distortion is taking a fact and making it mean whatever the person needs to have it mean. The erosion of character armor enables the person to become aware of her distortions and begin to correct them.

8. The patient has the emotions and feelings. If the therapist provides the words and ideas, the patient expresses her feelings and thus validates what she is experiencing.

9. Distance is the ability to look at yourself as if you were someone else whom you know very well. The patient is no longer overwhelmed and now has distance as she and the problem become two separate entities.

Take, for example, a person who had frequent anxiety attacks. Before treatment, the patient and the anxiety attacks were one. The patient was the anxiety attack. In the process of standing off and studying the anxiety attacks by using the conceptualizations the therapist has given, the patient begins to feel something alien is exploiting her. She tries to find out why she is being used, what it is all about. Doing that, in itself, has a curative effect because she is introducing the self, mind, will, and self-decision which stand on one side against the anxiety attacks on the other. She is not entirely helpless. There is a chance she can do something which in itself gives her courage or fortitude. It has a temporary curative effect.

NOTES

1. Wilhelm Reich, *Character Analysis*, 3d enlarged ed., Theodore P. Wolfe, trans., Noonday Press (New York: Farrar, Straus and Giroux, 1969).
2. Ibid., p. 41.
3. Ibid., p. 44.
4. Ibid., p. 47.
5. J. P. Chaplin, *Dictionary of Psychology*, revised ed., Laurel Editions (New York: Dell, 1984), p. 104.

3

Relationship and Therapeutic Involvement

RELATIONSHIP

In this chapter relationship refers to the positive beneficial connections between human beings. They are entered into and maintained by choice. A relationship is like a bridge over which traffic from both sides travels openly and freely. My feelings, thoughts, and reactions go to you and yours come to me. I do not think there is such a thing as a negative relationship. I see them as involvements which are defined later on.

What is a relationship? As far as I know, there is no definition of an emotional relationship between human beings. There are discussions about how to describe such a relationship but no definition that makes it understood as a distinctive behavioral phenomenon.

There are many kinds of relationships doing all different types of things. A relationship is undefined but understood by knowing what it does or by what happens in one. The person who knows what the relationship does knows how to use it for the other's benefit as well as her own or stay away from it because of the harm it creates.

Many emotions and feelings cannot be shared. They are in you and that is where you begin and end. You cannot feel another's pain or pleasure. Others experience them differently. You can empathize with them in terms of how you experienced those emotions. I cannot feel your headache, but I know how I felt when my head hurt and imagine you are feeling something like that, too. We are born alone, to a great extent live alone, and we die alone. We deny the aloneness in our lives when we talk about relationships.

A relationship is every person's search to counteract the natural basic loneliness of life. Your skin divides you from other people, from your family. You are alone. A relationship brings one nearer to another person and helps us feel that we are not isolated. We think about ourselves when we are alone and are more liable to become depressed. We tend to think about death, catastrophe, and the unpredictability of existence. A relationship is a way of knowing or finding out that other people have the same or similar troubles. You share in humanity's lot and are like other people.

A relationship is not based on responsibility. Responsibility is a judgment word carrying in it a sense of duty or owing. In a relationship I do not owe you anything because I feel you are a part of me and I want to take care of me. I give because I want to. You feel the same way about me, without any exceptions on either side. You are not expected to do anything in a relationship. The word *expect* imposes an idea of what should happen in a relationship. People say if you want something to happen between you and another person you must put something in it. "Have to" and "want to" stand for imposed ideas. In a relationship either something happens or it does not. In his essay "Of Friendship," Michel de Montaigne tried to explain why he loved his friend but he felt unable to do so except by answering: "Because it was he, because it was I."[1]

A relationship involves taking a chance emotionally with another person. All human relationships are based on the faith that the other person we are attached to will not try to destroy us. If that trust is lacking, especially between a man and a woman, then something is very wrong.

Life is full of danger. On one level of a relationship, the two of you are going to share the danger. What affects one of you affects the other. Only one of you may be at risk, but both of you have to live with the endangered one's attempts to cope with the trouble. If you get sick, I will take care of you. If it is contagious, I have to take the chance of catching it also.

INVOLVEMENT

An involvement is using a person for your own ends with little or no regard for his needs or feelings. It can be illustrated by how we take care of matches. We keep them dry, away from heat, in a safe place. We take care of them until we are ready to use one to light a fire. The match head is struck and flares up. The fire is lit. Having no further use for the match, we blow it out and throw it away. So it is in an involvement with a person.

Most relationships are involvements in varying degrees. One or both parties are using the other person to some extent to get what they want. This is especially so in those situations in which one or both of them is emotionally disturbed. An example is the marriage in which a fearful spouse dominates so as not to feel afraid and the other permits it all the while hating the domination, but needing to feel wanted. A relationship free of involvement is not a common occurrence.

Relationship and Therapeutic Involvement

In psychotherapy the beginning connection between therapist and patient is that of an involvement. The patient pays the therapist to give him some relief, temporary or permanent, from emotional problems. Ideally, the therapist has a hunger to do psychotherapy but needs a patient to satisfy it and at the same time earn a living. Whenever a therapist relieves a person of pain, he sees the practitioner belonging to him as an extension of himself. He will not let the therapist go. A relationship has begun and is interrelated with the involvement.

A person continues in treatment because she feels she is getting something out of it. The therapist puts the responsibility on the patient to become involved by telling her, "I don't know what your problem is. You're the only one who knows, but you don't know it yourself. I know, with your help, how to find out what it is, but you have to help me. I have certain methods to get at

it. I will tell you these methods and you have to work at it. If
you don't help me to help you then you may as well not continue
as you will be wasting your time and money." In the attempt to
discover what the patient's problem is, the therapeutic involvement is born.

In a therapeutic involvement, a person's emotions encase an
idea in the same way as a ring encases a diamond. The ring is
the setting for the diamond. The setting in a therapeutic involvement is the emotions triggered by an idea. At first, patients
try to look at the problem intellectually. Usually, they do not
know what the problem is. This degree of involvement is no
guarantee that eventually they will begin to interact with their
problems. The second level of therapeutic involvement is the
patients' awareness of what is going on emotionally and reacting
to it because intellectually their therapists have called it to their
attention. By sheer repetitive talking and getting the patients
intellectually engaged in the problem, they begin to look at themselves. They get excited, upset, angry, or whatever by what they
see.

With a therapeutic involvement, treatment can now begin.
Patients are emotionally engaged with their problems and the
attempts they and their therapists are making to either reduce
or resolve them. Everything that happens in treatment now has
a positive or negative emotional impact on patients and helps to
bring about modification.

The Difference in an Organization

In an organization a patient is called a client, a person who
comes in off the street and says, "I want you to help me." Organization refers to any group established to help people with
their emotional problems, although they may offer aid in other
areas as well. In that setting, a person is also a statistic. To the
administrator, the client is more important as a statistical entity
than as someone needing help. This is also true, to a degree, to
the practitioner giving the service. Unless enough people use
the organization, both administrator and practitioner may lose
their jobs. That means within the context of the organization's
purpose both practitioner and client have to achieve certain
things in a specified time. The practitioner has a quota of people

to see and must keep costs down. Each client can get only a limited amount of time. There is a pressure on both to produce quickly and cheaply. This limits the degree of relationship and therapeutic involvement possible which stunts treatment.

Therapeutic Involvement Creates the Relationship

Therapists put a great deal of emphasis on the therapeutic relationship and neglect the therapeutic involvement. Practitioners believe a therapeutic involvement can come out of a relationship, but actually a relationship comes from the therapeutic involvement. An example of this is two people whose jobs call for their working together. They are trying to repair a car. One works under the car and the other passes in tools as they are called for. In the beginning, as long as one helps the other to do what each one has to do, nothing more is required. Over a period of time they study each other and begin to react to each other's moods, work patterns and rhythms, habits, attitudes, emotions, and ideas. These reactions create the relationship. A flow of feelings and emotions begins to travel freely back and forth between them through the framework of their mutual job involvement. The relationship can be parallel to or accompany the involvement, but the involvement comes first.

Similarly, this is what happens in psychotherapy. The therapist and patient come together to reduce or resolve the patient's problems. Each of them must do his part. The patient enters treatment to achieve a certain purpose with the help of the therapist or to arrive at an alternate goal. If the therapist is to help, the patient has to do what is needed. The therapist has to put the patient into a therapeutic setting by explaining what they are trying to do, how it is done, the theory behind it, and the patient's part in it. Eventually the patient feels or says, "This is like preparing me for an operation." Out of their mutual involvement in working together the relationship evolves.

Beginning the Relationship

What the Therapist Does

First, the therapist does not try, early in treatment, to have the patient fully realize how sick he is. The therapist waits until the relationship is strong enough to provide the support the person needs because such knowledge increases the patient's anxiety.

Second, the therapist avoids a contest of wills, which the patient always wins, provided she does not try to dictate how the therapist shall do psychotherapy. The practitioner always has the last word about treating the patient.

Third, the therapist pays close attention not only to what the patient says but also how she says it. It is indicative of the way the individual has learned to relate to another human being. In the beginning, the therapist goes along with how the person relates so that the patient is not frightened by treatment and runs away.

Fourth, as much as possible, the therapist should see only the patient so that he has no question the therapist is there for him.

Knowing and Understanding

The patient must feel the therapist understands her. Knowing is an intellectual comprehension of the facts. Understanding is knowing the facts plus their meaning and a feeling for their place in the total situation. Understanding is retrospective as it takes place after the experience. It also implies a reciprocal relationship. The person you understand also understands you and responds to you because he knows that you know how he feels. Understanding, therefore, applies only to people. You may be able to feel with an inanimate objective thing or another life form such as a dog or fish, but that is using empathy rather than understanding.

The Use of Understanding with a Depressed Person. During treatment one of my patients sat like a piece of wood and could not talk. I was able to break through by telling her exactly what was happening. In that sense I became the only other person in the world who existed. She existed but she felt dead. Now there was another person who knew how she felt—me. The fact that she felt there was one more person besides herself helped her to get out of her deep depression. Step by step I was able to explain to her how she felt, and she realized I knew.

Beginning Therapeutic Involvement

A therapeutic involvement means patients talk with their therapists about what they do not understand and cannot discuss with anybody else. They invest their emotions in their therapists. They trust the practitioners enough to tell them what is really bothering them. They are afraid or ashamed to tell somebody else. They give therapists their innermost thoughts and feelings, expecting them to accept these graciously. They hope practitioners will give them back something that helps them to either weaken or remove whatever thoughts and feelings bother them. When patients open up emotionally, therapists have to get a wedge in to keep them open. A wedge is anything practitioners do to keep patients from forgetting or avoiding what was uncovered.

The therapeutic involvement comes as patients continue in treatment and begin to see what is in it for them. Involved patients change their whole attitude to treatment. Involved means patients want to be on their therapists' side instead of remaining on opposite sides. These patients feel that if their therapists want something, they must either give it to them or they will be the losers. At first, patients begin to give their therapists something very little, testing to see what they do with the material.

In dealing with any patient, the practitioner has to have the therapeutic involvement and relationship work together. If the two of them are able to say they like each other then they have a relationship but not a therapeutic involvement. When the therapist works hard at getting the patient to like her, that is creating a relationship. When the practitioner concentrates on what the patient is doing with her, that is creating an involvement. The therapist should let the patient do the work and not try to do most of it for him. That is how patients get involved. Everything the therapist does in the first few interviews is an abstraction. The patient concretizes the abstraction by injecting it with his experiences which makes the person become therapeutically involved. Then the therapist and patient have both a relationship and a therapeutic involvement based not on time spent together but on what happens in the session.

Therapists should exemplify what they are talking about, using example after example. Practitioners should not just talk about an intervention. They or their patients should do it. They should have patients experience what they are talking about. Patients should begin to wonder what is going to happen next, but therapists should not tell them in advance.

Assignments Involve Patients in Therapy

One way to involve a person in her therapy is to give her assignments, things to do outside of the treatment session that increase her awareness of the problem. Most people do not like the idea of just talking with a therapist. There are a lot of people they can talk to. They want to participate, be active, do something. It is especially true with people who have much emotional pressure inside them. Activity gives them a more satisfying outlet for reducing that pressure than talking. An example of an assignment is asking the patient to make notes on what happens when she is unable to tell someone what she wants or to keep count of how many times she became angry in one day.

At times, patients are quite spiteful. When I give an assignment I let the patient know I doubt if he will do it. This makes him feel he has to prove to me he can do it, in spite of what I said.

When to Give Assignments

1. When patients are not emotionally involved in their therapy; when an intellectual curiosity brings them back each time.
2. When the patient is more a doer than a talker.
3. As a way of bypassing a resistance that keeps the patient from getting involved in her therapy.
4. Do not give assignments to patients who believe in logic, will, and such intellectual approaches. Since they have placed their faith in logic and will, they believe they can do whatever they want if they put their minds to it. By giving such people assignments therapists help them to exercise their will and logic which strengthens their pathology.

Involving a Patient in Therapy

First, by coming to see a therapist, the patient is in process of becoming aware of herself. The therapist should recognize the person's increasing self-awareness and point it out to the patient.

Second, something happens in every session. The therapist should watch for it and call the patient's attention to it.

Third, when the therapist compares a current session to a previous session, there is usually an increase in the patient's awareness which the therapist should point out.

Fourth, the patient's interest in himself involves him in his treatment. The therapist should support that self-interest as many times a patient fears he is too self-centered.

Fifth, listening back to a selected part of a tape recorded session is another way to involve a person in therapy. I discuss this intervention in Chapter 4. The therapist assumes the patient is experiencing what he is talking about, especially a very upsetting experience. Many times the patient feels nothing. He hears himself as the tape recorder is played, talking coolly about a highly dramatic encounter and then becomes very disturbed. He has begun to let himself know there was more to the experience than he wanted to realize.

Some Conditions Affecting the Degree of Relationship and Therapeutic Involvement

Wants. All human desires can be broken down into the two categories of what a person wants and does not want. The strength and direction of those longings affect the degree to which the patient establishes a relationship and involvement with the therapist.

Characteristic and Uncharacteristic. The combination of the patient's natural tendencies and the fear of being so open determines how much and how soon she enters into a relationship and involvement. The therapist must realize and accept that the patient's character is unchangeable. A naturally reserved person is not going to become an aggressive salesperson.

The Level on Which They Work. When the therapist works on the surface with the patient, the connection between them is mostly relationship with some involvement. If the therapist works with the patient's unconscious, there is an intense relationship between them and great involvement in the therapy.

Counterproductive Relationships. Sometimes a relationship can counteract a therapeutic involvement. This happens when the patient emphasizes the relationship with the therapist instead of what they are supposed to be doing. Some patients have such a need to please their therapists that they fool practitioners into thinking they are healthier than they are. These patients give their therapists what they think the practitioners want which does nothing toward resolving the problem.

Gender Difference. Every male therapist has difficulties in working with women because a man cannot fully understand a woman. The same applies to a female therapist working with a man. Because of cultural conditioning, a woman's relationship to the world is different from a man's. Her functions in life are unlike his. He cannot bear children. Her difference in body makes a difference in her feeling and thinking. Nonetheless, it is not a foregone conclusion that women should work with female therapists and men with males. It simply needs to be recognized that a therapist of the opposite sex has to work harder to understand and establish a relationship and involvement with a patient. Their common humanity enables them to understand each other. In some instances, it is better if the patient has a therapist of the opposite sex. In working with a man, a woman learns about her own men, how to deal with them, and a great deal about herself in relation to men.

Other Contacts. The fewer the contacts with people close to the patient or her family members, the less the relationship is threatened by the patient's suspicions and jealousies.

Dreams. In the beginning, many of the patient's dreams are about the relationship and involvement with the therapist. Dreams give the therapist some idea of what is happening between them and the patient. The dreams can be used to strengthen the therapeutic connection.

The Therapist's Ability to Tolerate a Patient's Pain. Emotionally upset people compulsively go in directions they feel they should not. They know what they are doing but cannot stop themselves. Instead of warning them, therapists should wait until patients hurt enough to begin questioning what is happening. Then they can participate in what their therapists are trying to do to help them. Such participation involves patients in their therapy. After a treatment session, therapeutically involved patients think about what happened instead of just talking, walking out, and forgetting it.

THE THERAPEUTIC NEED FOR RELATIONSHIP
AND INVOLVEMENT

To Use Interventions

The explanations the therapist gives are usually related either to the questions the patient asked or might ask. Explanations about what the patient is interested in help to involve her in treatment. In this way the therapist establishes an intellectual basis with the patient for what they are trying to do.

The therapist should not use the interventions until there is an intellectual understanding with the patient about their use or until the patient becomes involved. When the patient becomes involved in what the therapist is doing and feels it is important, she will establish a relationship with the therapist. This makes the therapist very important to the patient and gives any intervention used its greatest impact.

To Begin to Work with Feelings

Intellectually patients can say, "Well, I think this is so or so," and it does not involve them very much. They can easily change their minds. But when they feel something, their whole personalities are involved. They have to have a relationship because when they tell their therapists how they feel about something, to a degree they trust them. These patients are giving therapists an insight into themselves.

The therapist must wait until a relationship is established with the patient. Even then, the practitioner does not ask, "How do you feel?" He begins intellectually by asking, "What do you think about your wife? How does she strike you?" Or the therapist could say, "Try to imagine yourself when you first met her, when you first saw her. Can you recall what your thoughts were?" The patient may say, "No," but will try. There is little danger of arousing the patient's resistance while the therapist digs into a situation he wants to explore. Exploring enables the practitioner to discover many unknown emotional factors.

Neurosis, Fantasy and Psychosis

The child in his mother's womb does not need a relationship because it is a part of the mother. A relationship starts when the umbilical cord is cut. The child needs a relationship to survive on his own. Crying and noise making are his way of getting what he needs to survive. Actually, the child gets what he wants without giving anything; things come to him on demand. As the child grows older, his parents have a relationship on two bases: (1) because the child is an extension of themselves and (2) because it is their duty.

The child continues to grow and experiences a relationship as a feeling of omnipotence. Either the parents discipline the child and make him give something for what he gets or the child gets his own way and continues to be omnipotent. The usual arrangement is the child being told, "If you are good [i.e., do what I want you to do], then this is what you will get. If you don't do it, you don't get what I could give you. Eat your supper and I will let you have your dessert." Omnipotence comes out of the child's feeling he can disregard eating supper and get dessert anyway.

When a child goes out into the world feeling omnipotent, he is frustrated because the world does not react as parents would. The world says, "If there is to be something happening between us, it must be a mutual give and take, not one-sided." The omnipotent person feels this is asking for more than the world has a right to expect. The world says, "Then you don't get anything from me."

The child then becomes neurotic; the emotions he freely expressed to his parents become congealed. A congealed emotion is an emotion that gets stuck in the process of expression. Becoming neurotic makes the child more susceptible to psychosis. As the child continues living in touch with the world at large, he becomes extremely frustrated because he needs more and gets less. Since he cannot get what he needs, or wants, or thinks he needs, he lives in fantasy. Either the child has somebody who controls him in some way so that fantasies do not proliferate or living in fantasy becomes a way of life. Eventually he cannot tell the difference between reality and fantasy; this inability to distinguish is a psychosis.

Generally, therapists use their relationship with patients to get all the emotions out into the open. If the preceding description is correct, however, they are doing just the opposite of what they should do. A therapist who gets all the emotions out into the open is enabling the patient to revert to feeling and behaving omnipotently again. The person feels she can say or do whatever she wants without giving anything of herself. This is the way the child behaved with her parents. If the patient, on the basis of experience with the therapist, believes she can behave the same way with strangers, the practitioner has put this person on the road to a psychosis. In the world, people do not accept the omnipotent feelings and behavior. They rebuff the person who retreats into fantasy. This is what happens when the therapist has a relationship without the patient's involvement in the treatment, which requires the person giving of herself. The patient does not change, stays in treatment, and may become psychotic.

To Cope with Regression

While in treatment, the patient may regress for many reasons. Sometimes the person becomes prepsychotic. The bond to the therapist and the understanding of what they are trying to do holds the patient together until a less stressful time is reached. It helps prevent a psychosis. The relationship with the therapist enables the patient to feel liked and accepted no matter how she feels and behaves. The involvement in treatment is not lost at such a time. Having an understanding of what is happening and what to do helps keep the person oriented. The patient continues making the effort, as best she can, to give the therapist whatever is needed to help her.

To Help Patient Renunciation

Change in psychotherapy means the patient has to let go of those emotions and feelings that were making her ill and let something more beneficial take their place. For a patient to give up something, the therapist must have a very strong relationship with the person and the patient must feel she is getting something in return. There are other factors to consider, but these two are the most important.

To Change Habits and Attitudes

To counteract an attitude, a person has to change his habits. To establish new habits, a person has to be involved in a reality which makes their acquisition necessary. In the process of doing, time takes over and creates the habit which modifies the attitude. If the therapist can get the patient actively involved in treatment, the person feels and behaves differently. This counteracts the patient's pathology.

When the patient finds that she can do an activity she could not do before, she is not as constricted as she once was. The performance gives the patient confidence in herself and changes her attitude. The patient may say, "Look, I can't do this. I'm all upset about this and that." The therapist should take the patient into the area of her upset and fantasize the upset in the session. The practitioner should have the patient visualize the situation and talk about what she is doing. The therapist suggests, "Okay, you hate to wash dishes; but you live alone, and no one is going to do them for you. There are no clean dishes left. Right here and now, let's wash dishes in your mind." After the patient does this the therapist says, "When you go home don't tell yourself you're going to feel better about it, but examine yourself while you wash dishes and see what happens." Attitudes can be changed only in proportion to changes in habits, and vice versa.

To Reduce Fear

While confronting an emotional problem by oneself, it is entirely possible that emotions, feelings, and thoughts may be triggered that one is afraid to face. In the presence of the therapist with whom the patient has a therapeutic relationship and involvement, however, this fear is reduced enough to enable the person to do that which he could not do alone. This is one of the obvious benefits of therapy usually not touched on.

NOTE

1. Michel de Montaigne, *Montaigne Selected Essays*, Charles Cotton and William Hazlitt, trans., Modern Library (New York: Random House, 1949), p. 65.

4

The Major Interventions

INTRODUCTORY REMARKS

An intervention is anything the therapist does that triggers an emotional reaction furthering the therapeutic process. Its purpose is to accentuate what happens or make something happen. The practitioner's evaluation of the treatment situation determines which intervention is used.

Interventions are something done from outside the patient to affect how the person feels and acts and to start a healing process. It is comparable to the use of crutches. The patient needs to walk but cannot without crutches, so they are supplied. The person can throw them away when they are no longer needed.

An intervention may be an open, direct effort by the therapist to suggest, motivate, and finally have the patient do something so there is movement in the situation. Intervening on that level does not involve unconscious material. It deals with the present and takes into consideration future implications. It works within narrow limits of predictability, based on the therapist's experience with the patient. It tries to answer the question, "How much more can the patient do now if she makes an effort?"

An example of this was a patient who was ready to leave a mental hospital. The whole process, from the hospital to his final return to work, included a number of interventions. The patient was afraid to leave the hospital grounds. The therapist asked the person to help move some equipment to her car, which was outside the grounds. The patient did so. Following that, the patient was fearful of driving. There was a need to intervene so he could drive off the hospital parking lot. The therapist had the person drive his car around the hospital grounds with the therapist as a passenger. The practitioner made use of other interventions to enable the patient to move into an apartment and resume working.

The relationship between patient and therapist is obviously important in using an intervention because the effort that the patient makes includes the desire to please the therapist. It also involves a feeling of growth on the part of the patient. Growth manifests itself as a need for movement. The patient feels he wants to do something but does not know what. Here it is difficult for the therapist to make a mistake because the intervention is a form of doing. Even if the doing does not exactly fit the patient's need at that particular point, it involves activity which the patient may discard and substitute with something more appropriate.

An intervention is an attempt to have the patient join the therapist against the destructive part of the person's unconscious. Instead of sitting and waiting for the unconscious to produce material to work with, which at times is important, the interventions are conscious attempts to help the patient by triggering unconscious material. The therapist's goal is to involve the patient in the intervention so they work together. In that way, patients participate in their own treatment. Not only can they think, feel, and experience, but they are also doing. They are the actors in their own dramas.

Before therapy, the patient had fleeting glimpses of her mysterious inner life. Now she is discovering those glimpses and making use of them. Interventions give the patient many opportunities to cooperate with the therapist. The therapist tells the patient what to do or look for. The patient then reports on what happened; participation is the name of the game. This is why therapy begins with a gradual intellectual commitment. The patient first understands what she and the therapist are trying to do; why such an intervention is used. It is a game, one that is not being played on the person but with the person. The difference in results are promising. It helps the patient to discover what she is feeling has been triggered by certain thoughts or emotions she was holding back.

Uncovering the Past

Uncovering the past is interesting but does not lead anywhere. Such knowledge is intellectual. It does not change the patient's emotional reactions, although it may explain his behavior in the present. The person has to relive what happened to him in the past and know emotionally that he is reacting to the present as if it were the past again. This means only those aspects of the past need to be looked at which are continuing to determine patient behavior in the present. This is why I do not concentrate on personal history, even though it is important for understanding the patient. Patients can get so lost in their pasts that they forget why they are seeing a therapist.

Functions

An intervention is not a trick, a gimmick, or a means of obtaining quick results. It deals with small fragments of surface behavior. Its two main purposes are explained below.

Its first function is to create a set of circumstances to erode character armor. An intervention is equal to therapy. It triggers the forces that do the eroding. The pathology is in the armoring in that the armor contains unacceptable emotions and feelings within an arrangement of prohibitions and behaviors. Erosion allows the strangulated emotions imprisoned in the character armor to come to the fore and creates a problem of acting out. Acting out occurs when the patient has strong feelings she is unable to express except by doing. An example of this is the angry person punching holes in doors or walls. The reduction of acting out is one of the important proofs that the successful use of an intervention is therapy. The intervention helps the person to become aware of what he is feeling which enables him to talk about it instead of doing something. The gradual disappearance of the acting out indicates the problem is on its way to eventual resolution.

The second function of intervention is to regulate the release of emotions so that they are in the service of psychotherapy. It is like drilling for oil and then regulating its flow after the oil is struck.

An emotional disorder is a form of damming comparable to a completely closed dam. The problem is to open the flood gates gradually so that the pent-up water does not inundate and destroy land and people in its rush to the sea. The interventions are a way to slowly open the gates within the patient so that there is a gradual flow of emotions. No one intervention can destroy the patient's defenses because each intervention triggers a piece of emotion and/or behavior small enough so that the patient can cope with it.

Using Interventions

Sometimes interventions are more important for the therapist's sake than for the patient. They reduce the practitioner's anxiety by giving her something to use or try instead of just groping in the dark. The interventions are ways the therapist can improvise within the method. The therapist should use the intervention when the patient understands intellectually what is being attempted. The interventions should be used only when working on the surface is not enough. The therapist should try to stay on the surface because it is always dangerous to go deeper. If change is achieved by working on the surface, the assumption is the change will stay.

A Scientific Experiment

The intervention is an attempt to test a psychotherapeutic theory without harming the human being. The use of silence as an intervention exemplifies this point. There is a difference between silence as a part of resistance and silence as an intervention. As a resistance, silence is considered an expression of hostility toward the therapist. Silence as an intervention is encouraged by the therapist as a means of triggering the unconscious. The therapist uses it to determine what the patient is feeling. As an intervention, silence simulates a laboratory experiment. The therapist is trying to discover if her theory can find support or is negated by the material produced by using silence. The same principle applies in all interventions used.

The Extent of an Intervention

The therapist should start with the assumption that the patient knows more about himself than the practitioner does. The patient enters treatment because he knows about himself, but at the same time, he does not want to know about himself. If by using an intervention the therapist can trigger an awareness of what prevents a patient from knowing about himself, she has done enough. Patients start thinking and asking questions, giving the therapist an idea of what questions to ask. The end result is more emotions are triggered at a rate with which the patient can live.

Can Interventions Contaminate or Condition?

The interventions do not condition or contaminate the patient. Should a therapist use interventions to trigger the unconscious and say the patient is conditioned, she is saying that she and the interventions are stronger than the patient's unconscious. Nothing is stronger than the unconscious. Therefore, the patient's unconscious cannot be contaminated. When the therapist works in a way to keep the therapeutic situation open ended, contamination or conditioning of any kind does not occur.

Aftereffects of Using an Intervention

Reactions to an Intervention

Usually, the patient's first reaction to an intervention is positive. An intervention suggests, asks, or tries to motivate the patient to do something. This is easier than grappling with intangible material where the patient does not feel as much in control. Doing, as compared with feeling or thinking, uses a knowledge and control the person is assumed to already have. This tends to make the patient cooperative.

Most negative reactions contain positive elements that can be used very effectively. For example, take the intervention of handshaking at the beginning and end of a session used with one patient. On the surface, it appeared innocuous. The first reaction was positive. The patient could understand and accept handshaking as a means of creating a much needed warmer relationship between himself and the therapist. A little later on, there was a strong negative reaction. It had brought to the fore the patient's anxieties about engaging in a close relationship. These reactions, as they were dealt with, helped to create a more intense relationship. The positive reaction was more or less taken for granted; the negative reaction was the most beneficial in the long run.

Based on my work with patients having character disorders, I see no other way of treating such people except with the use of interventions. Otherwise, the treatment of character disorders becomes an endless and perhaps insoluble problem. I have found interventions both necessary and effective.

The Danger of an Intervention

A good deal of control is exercised by the therapist in determining which interventions to use, when, and how. A similar control does not exist as emotions are released. There is no way to gauge the extent to which an intervention will affect a person. Further, trying to control the rate of emotional release is self-defeating as the usual result is to stop any release from happening. This raises the possibility of an intervention triggering emotions leading to a prepsychotic state. The use of an intervention depends on how secure the therapist feels. Whenever patient and therapist feel that a great deal has happened to modify the patient's life in a positive way, the therapist is in a position to take a chance. It is a gamble because there is no way to absolutely predict the possible positive gains or negative repercussions resulting from the intervention.

The therapist must learn which interventions are safe and effective for a particular patient. The patient is encouraged to react and explain how she is affected by a particular intervention. She thus becomes involved in her own therapy and at the same time gives the therapist an opportunity to become aware of progress or retrogression.

An intervention must do something or else it is useless for treatment purposes. Either it does something when used or it gives the therapist some assurance it could have an effect in the future. When the same interventions produce the same or similar effects in patients the therapist can determine which interventions are helpful and which to discontinue because they are harmful. This avoids the sudden leap from neurosis to psychosis because therapists have a good idea of what is happening to patients.

THE INTERVENTIONS

Silence

The Use of Silence

Silence is introduced to the patient and made a subject of mutual exploration. The kind of silence the therapist is trying to help the patient achieve is called a hypnagogic reverie. It is a sleepy or drowsy state in which the patient no longer controls what her mind thinks. It feels as if she is dreaming. I ask the patient to put her mind in neutral, as if it were an automobile engine running unconnected to the car's transmission. She is to let her mind go anywhere it wants and not control its direction. I explain that we are trying to find out what the patient is feeling, to help her learn what she wants. Her feelings tell her what she likes and dislikes, what is and is not important.

The therapist asks her to tell him whatever thoughts occur as the person sits quietly. It is the self watching and reporting on the self. Her thoughts carry the emotions and feelings she is experiencing. For instance, a person does not usually say, "I am angry." Instead she may talk about hitting someone. The thought carries the angry feelings. When the therapist has enough thoughts, an emotional pattern emerges or the practitioner intuitively recognizes what the underlying feeling is. Then the therapist decides how to use the information the patient has given him.

Even if the person knows what the therapist is trying to do, they may not be able to use being quiet for some time because he resents silence. He wants to talk since he understands psychotherapy is a talking cure. That is what he pays the therapist for. Why come to the therapist's office to be quiet? The answer is, "That's right; you can be quiet at home. Here in this session you're using talking to get away from what you are really thinking and feeling which is what we want to know. You couldn't discover what was happening inside you at home. You just sat there and learned nothing. Eventually, something will happen here as you sit quietly and tell me the thoughts you are having." The highest point of progress in the talking cure is arrived at when both patient and therapist are comfortable and participate in as well as communicate with each other's silence.

The use of silence may be nondirectional, as in free association, when the therapist asks the patient to just sit quietly and report the thoughts he has. This approach is usually used when the patient reports he has nothing to talk about and the therapist does not think it is the right time to explore specific problematic aspects of the person's behavior. Or it may be directional in that the therapist suggests what the patient should associate to. Silence is used directionally when the therapist has an idea of what the patient is experiencing or thinks some emotions and feelings have been stirred up that the person should know about. This approach helps the person learn what is happening inside emotionally.

When the patient uses silence comfortably, the hope is that to some extent she can free associate. Then the mind is like a glacier indiscriminately carrying along everything in its path. It may dredge up gold nuggets of awareness or a muck of chaotic impressions. Once the patient finds out what is there, then she—not the therapist—decides who she is and what she is going to do about what she wants.

There is no exact time to begin to use silence. The therapist must sense how soon after the beginning of treatment to introduce the patient to sitting quietly. I have done this as early as the second session.

Finding Out What Is There. Language is frequently used to escape from emotions and feelings. The patient talks to avoid being quiet. When a person is quiet he becomes aware of what is going on inside. Many times patients cannot tolerate knowing what their emotional state really is. Inasmuch as there is no other way to communicate except through language, it is important that the patient be quiet, try to get hold of what he is thinking, and report it to the therapist. The patient knows that whatever he says is based on what is actually happening, not as a way to hide. The thoughts he tells the therapist tell both of them what is going on.

Sometimes it is not clear if patients are talking to evade silence or if this is their own roundabout way of getting somewhere. If the therapist uses silence prematurely, patients will let her know they are not finished; they still have more to say.

When a patient who has done something he should not have sits silently with a therapist with whom he has a relationship, he feels guilty. As the patient sits quietly, the silence becomes intense and he feels guiltier and guiltier. He may then tell the therapist what he did.

Introducing the Patient to Silence. The following introductions help patients become familiar with silence and be at ease with it. Which approach to use depends on how fearful the patient is. In subsequent sessions, the therapist can increase the length of silence based on her judgment of whether the patient should know what is happening emotionally and how much being quiet the patient can tolerate.

In any one of these introductions, the patient may report her mind is a blank. The therapist explains what is happening based on the assumption that the human mind never stops working. Given their mutual agreement to this assumption, the therapist tells the patient she has encountered her unconscious. For some reason, the person's unconscious felt trying to find out what the patient was experiencing was dangerous. Therefore, the unconscious is telling both the patient and therapist to get lost; no information will be given.

Where there is the least fear, the therapist asks the patient to report the thoughts that occur during a minute of silence. The practitioner watches the clock and tells the patient when to stop. Then the therapist summarizes the thoughts the person had and asks the patient if she can see any pattern in them. After that, the practitioner tells the person the order she saw in the thoughts. Sometimes there is not enough of a pattern yet and the therapist asks the patient to associate to a thought she had during the minute. The therapist chooses such a thought as much from intuition as from any theory she may have about the patient. Through these associations, the patient and practitioner get an idea of what the patient is feeling at that time. The whole purpose of the exercise is to demonstrate that the patient has feelings she is not aware of and this intervention brings them out. This arouses and sustains the person's curiosity about herself.

Where there is more fear, usually mixed with skepticism, the therapist asks the person for the first thought that comes to mind. Then she asks the patient, "What occurs to you about that thought?" The therapist is trying to familiarize the patient with the process of association and demonstrate its value for treatment. An example of this is the woman who thought about opening the laces on a male therapist's shoes. This led to undressing the therapist, which led to the woman's fear of the therapist and her willingness to pay a sexual ransom to not be hurt, which uncovered her general fear of men.

For the most fearful patient, the therapist simply asks him to sit quietly and listen to his thoughts. He does not have to report any of those thoughts unless it is something he wants to talk about. The purpose is to give control over the situation to the patient to reduce his fear. Eventually, with familiarity, the patient relaxes and in the following sessions begins to give the therapist more and more of his thoughts.

When Not to Use Silence. One of my patients revealed all his perversions, difficult as it was. I talked a lot instead of letting him do all the talking. When a person shares material that he is ashamed, embarrassed, or guilty about, the practitioner should say something and not sit silently afterward. The patient interprets the therapist's silence as being negatively judgmental. The person needs to know right away the practitioner still likes him, accepts him, and that all is well between them. I talked a lot not out of my anxiety but because I was sorry for the man. I wanted to help him to talk without so much pain.

When people come in very emotional and upset, they want to talk and do talk a great deal. Then the patients stop as if they have talked themselves out. If the therapist were to say, "How about keeping quiet for awhile?" that would be very dangerous as it would produce more emotion, when there is too much emotion already. It would put the patients in touch with additional emotion inside themselves. The emotion would feed on itself and become greater. An example of this is the person who is afraid but talks about the fear. Even though the fear may or may not be reduced, it does not get any greater. Simply letting oneself experience and think about the fear enlarges it.

The therapist should not ask someone who is feeling much emotional pressure to be silent. Sitting quietly puts a lid on the emotional pressure in the person and makes it quickly build up. As a result of the increased pressure, the patient has to do something to relieve it, either talk, faint, or have a psychotic break.

When a patient asks the practitioner questions—especially if this is not just a way of getting the therapist off the track—to use silence is to stop the flow. A practitioner who does not respond to a patient's questions implies his questions are not important. The therapist can find out more by a patient asking questions than in many other ways. Is her husband going to work himself to death? Is her son going to kill himself? These things are important to talk about. What could be more important? To use silence here is to tell the patient to shut up.

The Forms of Silence

It is the lot of therapists to be faced frequently with silence in the course of their work. This section discusses the different ways in which the patient and the therapist may make use of silence.

Reporting Thoughts. At the beginning of therapy, after the patient has found some relief from the pressure that brought her to the therapist's office, she reaches a point where it is difficult to talk because she feels she has run out of subject matter. The person has told her story; now what? It is a common experience for patients on the way to their therapists' offices to be appalled by the question, "What am I going to talk about today?" They do not want to be repetitious, as that seems foolish. The very thought of such a possibility in the presence of therapists whose respect they are seeking is frightening. They becomes anxious.

The patient expects to participate in and be exposed to psychotherapy as the talking cure. In the session, the person is still. She cannot talk. She tells the therapist her mind is a blank. There she sits, silent in her misery and pain, not knowing what to do.

This is even more terrifying to the money-conscious patient who feels that the therapist's fee has become a fine for not talking. Unless the therapist knows what to do, the situation becomes threatening and ominous for both of them. Time lengthens; minutes become eternities.

In despair, the therapist turns to technical ammunition and devices to combat the silence. Foremost among these battering rams is that faithful, long-cherished concept called resistance. The therapist tells the silent patient she is exhibiting resistance because of this, that, or the other thing and maybe if the person considers this, that, or the other thing the resistance would disappear. Two things may now happen. One is that the patient does what the therapist suggests and apparently, for the time being, the resistance disappears. Two, the person has a new word with which to defend herself. Now when she cannot talk she will tell the therapist that she is resisting. The attempt to overcome silence ends up in creating a hiding place for the patient. She has a reason for not trying to find out what she is thinking. How can she if she is resisting?

I have found a simple and effective way to reduce anxiety and the other effects silence has on the therapeutic relationship. I ask the patient to consider the possibility that if he could sit quietly and be comfortably silent something positive would happen. Just the fact that the therapist and patient are at ease while each is silently aware of the other is a form of communication that can be used effectively in the therapy. However, the person is told, that obviously is not happening now. He does not know or trust the therapist well enough. His remaining silent is natural under the circumstances. The patient is relieved and no longer feels different or an outcast.

Therapists tend to talk too much because they are scared. They feel if they just sit there and listen they are going to get swamped by the material the patient gives them. They do not know where the talking is going and become fearful because they cannot impose a direction on what the patient talks about. Therapists can sit quietly for a long time if they are comfortable while the other person is talking. Their job is to listen. Patients can sense the therapist feels at ease and unbend. The person relaxes and talks to explore a situation, one thought leading to another. Things begin to evolve without deliberately using silence.

If therapists can respect and be comfortable with silence, even though resistance is a part of it, patients could accept on an intellectual level the meaning of silence as another form of speech that can be utilized at times as effectively as speaking. Silence is language. There is the silence in which patients are angry at their therapists and just sit and glare, refusing to say anything. There are times when patients are afraid of what their therapists will think and so decide to say nothing but look re-laxed. Other times persons are silent out of fear, but look very tense, expecting some kind of an attack from their therapists. Some patients in great pain cannot bring themselves to talk about it, so they sit and cry or move restlessly. Each different kind of silence is a commentary on what is happening as the session proceeds.

There is a similarity between hibernation in the physical world and silence in the world of the psyche. Hibernation is life pur-posely retreating into itself because exposure to the environment would destroy it. Life retreats almost to the point of extinction where it remains until such time as it can assert itself again in its full vigor. This is similar to an undisturbed silence seen by the therapist in a session. The prevailing descriptions of such a silence are pregnant, brooding, creative, or productive. Such descriptions are indicative of a form of gestation. Something is attempting to stay curled up within itself and when ready will emerge. Something is being born. Silence here seems to suggest the symbol of the womb.

Body language continues throughout the silences. The person assumes a posture, has an expression on her face, remains still, moves at certain times in certain ways, all of which say something. The language is limited in its quantity and quality. There are some things that need words for their expression.

Sounds and Images. There are times when a person chokes up or cries because he lacks the words or words are inadequate for expressing what he feels. The patient does not know why he has this problem. The practitioner tells the person, "I don't know the source of your choking up or crying, but I do know how we can try to get the reason out into the open. As you sit quietly, if you have any picture or sound in your mind of anything at all describe it to me." The patient attempts to comply because sounds or images are usually there. It does not always work the first few times. When the patient can give the therapist something to work with, the two of them try to discover by association what the sounds and images refer to and from that deduce what the patient may be experiencing. This is one way the therapist gives the patient words and ideas with which to think and talk.

Adult Play Therapy. Adult play therapy encourages the patient to use her imagination while sitting quietly. The difference between adult and child play therapy is the retrospective feelings and attitudes in the adult. The adult has more, both in quantity and quality, to look back on and use than does the child.

Adult play therapy counteracts the patient's difficulty in using silence. The person may be asked to imagine he is a deep-sea diver and dressed as such. He is going down through the water to the bottom of the ocean. A telephone line connects the diver/patient to the therapist on board the ship. The patient is to tell what he observes. The person starts by reporting what he imagines he would see on the ocean's bottom, but it can soon become a report of what he is thinking.

In a later stage of treatment, patients dramatize various aspects of their unconscious that they had worked on previously. They create primitive, personal characters based on their understanding of themselves now. These characters are brought together in the form of a play so that as adults patients can act out in fantasy and bring to completion childhood frustrations. The aftereffect of this fantasy is a pressure to implement the new freedom from the frustration in reality. Experimentally, with discretion, patients apply their feelings of freedom to their present reality. To a degree, patients have used their unconscious instead of their unconscious using them. This ability to use the unconscious is one of the signs of returning health.

Naming is another variation of adult play therapy. Here the patient names an emotion or feeling that makes him behave inappropriately. For instance, a patient named his fearful, immature feelings "the little guy". The named emotions or feelings are treated as an entity to whom the patient turns to find out what is making him behave as he does. The person has put some distance between himself and his emotions and feelings and can now bear to look at them. The patient asked "the little guy" how he felt or what he thought about a particular situation to get an idea of what fearful, immature emotions or feelings were motivating him.

There is a difference between naming and not naming. As, for example, there is a different result between naming something anxiety and giving it the name of a specific fear. Anxiety is the unknown, diffused, self-consuming, internalized fear the patient tries to get away from, while it runs with her. The same reaction as a specifically named fear is attached to something the patient is afraid of, but can define, identify, and has some idea of how to cope with it. The difference between not naming and naming is the difference between no control and some control over the situation and herself. The degree of accurate naming, that is a naming which closely corresponds to the patient's inner and outer reality, determines the degree of control. A patient with omnipotent feelings greatly distorts both realities and so comes up with a name that gives him no control over himself or his circumstances.

The danger in using dramatization and naming lies in patients treating the characters they have created as if they were real aspects of the persons. Patients can get lost trying to deal with imaginary figures that are abstractions of the unconscious. Therapists should keep those characters tied back to actual experiences or behavior in patients' lives.

Using the Audiotape Recorder

The major use of an audiotape recorder in psychotherapy is patient self-confrontation. A treatment session is recorded and either selected parts or the whole session is played back to the person. The process is completed by the therapist and patient discussing and trying to understand the person's reactions to the played back material. All of the variations of this technique involve playing back some part of the psychotherapy session to the patient. This is the most objective presentation of themselves that patients ever have, because the machine portrays the situation as it actually happened. People are presented to themselves without a bias.

The problem in using self-confrontation is making it an emotional experience for the patient. The chief goal of the therapist is not to obtain factual material but emotional content. The aim is to confront the patient with selected parts of the interview, where the mode of verbalization, the inflection of the voice, the basic emotions and feelings are revealed. The therapist must enable the patient to experience, instead of intellectually know, any insight or awareness derived from self-confrontation. The mass of information contained in the playback of a complete psychotherapy session can so confuse patients that they do not know on what to concentrate. They tend to focus on what is least painful for them to know about themselves or to avoid emotional involvement by analyzing the information instead of reacting to it.

Playing back segments of tape in different sessions illustrating the same behavior has the greatest emotional impact on the patient. It is comparable to listening to a piece of music and its variations again and again and hearing something different each time until the music is as fully experienced as possible. There is no rule for how often therapists do this. It is a matter of trial and error, depending on how much of an effect previous self-confrontation has had. Therapists have to pick the right moment, when patients seem receptive to what their therapists are trying to help them see.

Cautions about Self-Confrontation

The tape should stay in the possession of the therapist. This prevents the person from listening to the recording when the practitioner is not available. In my experience, patients have experienced anxiety attacks listening by themselves.

In the early stages of treatment, listening back should be used sparingly and with great caution to test the patient's ability to confront herself. Premature self-confrontation is the psychological equivalent of rubbing the patient's face in her emotional vomit. The patient does not yet have enough distance from the problem to prevent exposure to the pathology from further infecting and overwhelming her. The emotional impact may hit her when she is not ready or able to deal with what becomes evident. This can increase anxiety to a level interfering with everyday functioning. The therapist has to judge the right time and aspect of her pathology that the patient can tolerate confronting.

The therapist should show as little reaction to a playback as possible. The more only the patient's reaction is obtained, the better. Practitioners who reveal a reaction to a playback are superimposing their idea of the taped material over their patients' impressions. Patients disregard what they hear to pay attention to what their therapists have heard.

Some therapists play back the contradictory statements their patients make, thereby using the tape recorder as a lie detector. This is harmful. Whether intended or not, these therapists are telling their patients, "Tell the truth or I will use your own words to convict you of lying." Generally, it is best to avoid playing back contradictory statements. Even when it is done for the best of reasons, it makes patients look and sound foolish and reinforces the negative feelings they already have about themselves. It makes them inhibited and resentful.

Playback should not be used blindly, without a reason. Self-confrontation in psychotherapy is as effective as the scalpel in surgery and as harmful if misused. Therapists must know why they are using playback, otherwise it may do more harm than good by triggering emotions and feelings that should have been left alone.

Therapists become so accustomed to using recorders that they overlook the possibility their patients may not like it. The use of the recorder assumes patients have a great deal of trust and confidence in their therapists. It is very important to check and find out if this so. Practitioners cannot assume their patients are comfortable enough to ask them not to record.

Therapeutic Uses of Recorders

This section describes how to choose certain tape segments for playback and how to use them therapeutically. Based on my experience, these suggestions are meant to be used by therapists as they see fit in treatment situations. In all of these playbacks, I asked patients to write down any thoughts that occurred to them as they listened and to report them at the end of the playback.

Self-confrontation is not a method of psychotherapy by itself but an intervention in its own right that may also be used to make other techniques and interventions more effective. Too-frequent use blunts its emotional impact. After too many exposures, the patient becomes as analytical as the therapist about the played back material, with little of the desired emotional involvement. When used occasionally, playback stands out. It signals to the patient that the therapist is trying to call attention to something that happened. Even if the patient does not have a reaction to the playback, he wonders after the session why the therapist made a particular selection, thus continuing the therapeutic process.

As an Objective Observer. The audiotape recorder serves as an equalizer between the patient and the therapist. Both of them are putting themselves on record. The patient may ask for a playback, but the final decision is up to the therapist. The only time a therapist may not refuse a patient's request for a playback is when there is a difference of opinion about what was said. Each has an equal right to listen to the recording as the final arbiter of what was said by whom. In that instance the tape recorder is used as an objective, corrective observer of both the patient and the therapist. The machine has saved the experience from oblivion.

To Gain Distance from Themselves. When patients listen back sufficiently, they eventually become two people, one of whom observes the other person on the tape. They catch the nuances in their voices the therapist misses. They hear emotions and feelings they were not aware of before. Their behavior becomes clearer to them. They are no longer overwhelmed as they listen to themselves struggle with their problems. By confronting themselves and coping with their reactions to what they hear, patients gain enough emotional distance from their difficulties to literally treat themselves. They begin to locate their pathology and try to get rid of it with direction from their therapists.

To Form a More Realistic Concept. Hostile patients frequently conceive of themselves as good-natured and accepting of others.

When self-confrontation exposes how angry they are, they may seek to change what they recognize as destructive behavior. They are struck by the fact that the persons delineated on the playback are not the same as the pictures they had of themselves. They realize they want to be loved, not disliked.

As such patients realize that their ideas about themselves do not coincide with their feelings and behavior, they begin to think about the kinds of people they are. They form a different, hopefully more realistic, conception of themselves which they verify by again looking at their feelings and behaviors as presented by playback.

To Validate the Therapist's Theory. Self-confrontation may be used to determine if any hypothesis the therapist has about the patient is correct. The patient hears herself and reacts to a playback. The reaction tells both the patient and therapist what is going on in the patient. Such a reaction should have been at least partially predicted by the therapist's hypothesis. If the reaction is unforeseen, the therapist should rethink how he sees the patient.

Tape selection for playback constitutes an interpretation by the therapist. The practitioner places emphasis on the behavior that he thinks exposes what motivates the patient. With a hostile patient, the therapist may hypothesize the hostility is triggered by the patient's feeling a rejection by the practitioner where none was intended. The therapist would then play back a tape segment containing inappropriately hostile behavior. The practitioner's first effort is to help the patient recognize and accept the hostility. Then the patient discusses his thoughts about hostility. The therapist listens to see if the person is feeling rejected and, if so, what it is based on.

To Separate the Past from the Present. It is highly unlikely that on a first playback the therapist can uncover what makes a hostile patient imagine a rejection, if this is what is happening. The person has to confront his hostility via playback and other methods a number of times. These interventions can trigger memories and feelings from the patient's past. Together, patient and therapist try to determine the meaning of those past experiences for the patient. The person may then realize that a current situation similar to one in the past does not mean he is being rejected again. This understanding alters the way the patient feels so that the behavior changes.

To Erode Character Armor. In the beginning of therapy, the patient's increased emotional awareness erodes the character armor that interferes with treatment. Playing taped segments helps a patient see the techniques symptomatic of his illness he uses to defend himself. The aim is to have the patient confront and question his need for such behavior and increase his desire for change through psychotherapy.

To Counteract Emotional Noninvolvement. Listening back is a way to counteract two parallel processes going on at the same time as the patient talks. In one process, the patient's talking temporarily relieves the emotional pressures she is feeling. Playback confronts her with those pressures again and brings out the need to resolve them on a more lasting basis. The other is an erasing process. It appears as if the person really feels what she was talking about, but many times this is not so. The patient needs to feel she did not say what she did, especially when she talks about painful or shame-producing subjects. She immediately forgets what she has said. Playback makes her very excited and upset because the original emotions and feelings that she talked about before the erasing process took place are reawakened for further treatment.

To Overcome Resistance. Extended playback is any playback that runs for more than five minutes. This form of self-confrontation overcomes a patient's massive resistance to looking at feelings. I select a session or long segment that mostly contains denied feelings or in which the resistance to awareness is very evident. I play a portion for up to 15 minutes in the same session. For a playback longer than that, I ask the patient to come back at a time when he can listen in my office to all of the particular session that highlights the feelings or the difficulty he has accepting them. He is left alone with the tape recorder, after having been shown how to operate it. I stay in an adjacent room in case he needs me. After he listens to the tape, we have a regular psychotherapy session beginning with the patient's reactions to what he heard. The prolonged exposure saturates the patient with what he is doing so that it becomes very hard not to know what is happening. In the ensuing discussion I try to help the patient become aware of what he is avoiding looking at.

To Amplify Feelings. Dreams, imagery, fantasies, memories, and associations can be played back to uncover any further feelings not revealed by previous discussion of the material. Playback creates a situation in which these aspects of the unconscious become emotional experiences instead of something to be accepted on faith. The person is confronted with material that is the concrete, chaotic, raw expression of her unconscious and reacts to it some more. Treatment becomes an adventure because who knows what the patient will come up with next or what the therapist will play back?

To Demonstrate Change. Playback can present patients with concrete evidence of how much they have changed. This is done by playing a segment from early in their treatment and then playing a piece from later on in their therapy that illustrates the difference in behavior. This means therapists must keep good records of what is on the tapes.

Integration by Reactivating Emotions and Summarizing

Integration: 1: the act, process, or an instance of integrating: The condition of being formed into a whole by the addition or combination of parts or elements. 2a: a combination of separate and diverse elements or units into a more complete or harmonious whole.[1]

This definition describes what has to happen in effective psychotherapy. Somehow the patient has to pull together all that he has learned about himself and use it in a way that is constructive and comfortable. One of the reasons psychotherapy takes so long is that the same material has to be gone over again and again because it is too painful to be absorbed easily. This intervention, by deliberately using repetition, reduces the overall need for it. Additionally, the patient resists including the awareness into the self because a painful emotional reorganization must take place to accommodate the new material. Summarizing sessions and reactivating emotions that have been forgotten are interventions for speeding up this process of assimilation.

Not only is there a problem of inclusion, but patients must also decide what they are going to do with what they now know. The tendency is to forget what they have learned and remain in the same old pathological groove. Applying their understanding creates new situations whose outcome they cannot predict. They enter into the unknown which is always frightening.

Reactivating Emotions

This intervention should be used as soon as the situation is stabilized, usually by the second or third interview. In a previous interview I explain why, beginning in their next session, my first question will be, "What do you remember of the previous session? Anything that occurs to you." When they do not remember at all, I ask, "What comes to your mind as the most important thing that happened in the last session?" I do this every session thereafter.

If the patient has forgotten, the therapist should not let her stew in not remembering. She should help the person by reminding her abstractly what happened so she is free to associate. The therapist should not be too concrete as that hems in the patient. This is done by giving the person clues about what was discussed. When nothing brings the memory back, the therapist should tell the patient what happened. As she remembers, other things may come tumbling out.

One of the ways patients let their therapists know that they have lost the emotions from the previous interview is by talking superficially or in a way that simulates emotionality. People try to confuse the therapist and themselves because they had to wipe out what happened in the last session. They cannot really erase it, but they have forgotten enough so that they are not so painfully affected by it. These patients are letting their therapists know a great deal was done, but they don't want to feel it. They are upset now and want the practitioners to leave them alone. The interview goes nowhere.

Therapists should use silence to reactivate emotions that have gone down below between interviews. They should ask patients to sit quietly and report what occurs to them about the material they forgot from the previous session. Frequently, the thoughts reactivate the forgotten emotion. Then therapists watch to see what patients do with the reawakened emotion; what they say about it, feel about it, and do with it.

Let us say that in session one an important emotion was triggered. In session two the patient reported he forgot what happened in session one, was told what happened, and through the use of silence reactivated the emotion. However, in session three the patient tells the practitioner he forgot session two. The therapist should not try to directly rekindle an emotion that has gone underground again but point out that the patient is staying away from something. Trying to reactivate it again increases the patient's resistance because he had to hide from the emotion in the first place. The therapist should try to trigger the emotion indirectly or make a mental note that this is an area due for further exploration at an appropriate time.

The Theory of Reactivating Emotions

The theory of reactivation assumes that after an interview the patient suppresses whatever was painful or unpleasant. What the person forgets gives the therapist a rough idea of what was painful enough so that the patient needed to lose it. If the therapist talks openly about forgetting, the person resents it because she may feel the practitioner thinks she is an idiot. The therapist has to learn what the patient tends to suppress and try to work directly with it. Sometimes the practitioner must dominate a session to find out what was so painful in the previous interview. Suppressing can happen one of two ways: either the patient remembers only the unimportant details of the last interview or she forgets the previous session entirely.

The very attempt to remember helps patients keep the session in mind for the next time. They feel they should remember. The fact that they forget makes a tremendous impression on them and spurs them to make a greater effort to remember thereafter, which makes an even greater impression when they forget.

Patients who remember what they talked about may take it further in the next session. They may have many associations to go with the recalled ideas and emotions. Frequently, patients come up with new associations in the next session that give their therapists access to their problems.

Functions

Reactivating emotions has at least three important functions. One is the recall that reinforces what happened in the previous session. Reactivating emotions attempts, by repetition, to strengthen the effect of the ideas or emotions that were experienced in a previous interview so they are not forgotten again and can be further considered. Many patients cannot come more than once a week, which is a long interval between sessions; reactivating emotions is one way to counteract that lapse of treatment.

The second function is the organizational effect of the recall. Bringing back ideas or emotions also ties a patient to, and gives her continuity with, what happened in earlier sessions. It organizes cumulatively what happened in the earlier session and connects it to the next one. It unites the person's life. The patient's whole life is reorganized by the continuous relationship between one interview and the next one.

Third, it reduces anxiety in that seeing where they came from gives patients a sense of direction to their lives and the feeling of having some control over where they are going.

Summarizing

There are two kinds of summaries. Content summarizing, as its name implies, simply sums up what the patient talked about. In the beginning, until the therapist has a relationship with the patient, this is the approach to use. Process summarizing refers to what the therapist saw happen to the patient emotionally during the therapy hour. The person can find this form of self-confrontation very threatening when he does not feel safe with the therapist. Usually, summarizing is a combination of these two approaches, with the therapist using her judgment as to which one to emphasize.

The therapist summarizes from the first session onward because the patient is covertly asking, "Do you know what happened today? Were you listening?" The therapist's summary answers these questions. Without summarizing some patients stop treatment because they do not have a sense of having accomplished anything.

Every summary must be based on one of the themes of the particular case. Without a theme the therapist is lost and cannot make a summary that furthers the treatment process because she does not know what to emphasize. See Chapter 5 for a discussion of case theory and theme.

When a therapist summarizes a session he may need to concentrate on the negative, painful aspects of what happened. As long as a relationship exists with the patient, no harm is done. The patient likes and trusts the therapist. Without the relationship, dwelling on the negative is like throwing garbage in the patient's face. In the beginning, the therapist should just barely touch on the negative experiences in a session until a relationship has developed.

At times during an interview the patient may spontaneously make connections and interpretations without any direction from the therapist. When this happens, the therapist should not summarize the session but leave it wide open with the implication that more is to come. No one knows ahead of time which way the patient is going to go with her insights. To some extent, a summary is an interpretation by the therapist who selects out of the interview what he, not the patient, thinks is important. It conditions the direction in which the patient's thoughts go and may shut some off.

Sometimes the patient simply relates events; not knowing what is going on, all the therapist can do is summarize what the person relates. As long as that happens only occasionally and the practitioner can point out where there is regression or some progress that is all right. Not knowing what is going on is not unusual unless it happens frequently. The therapist can end the session with a semicolon, leaving the patient to mull on the matter. If the therapist cannot summarize the session or does not know what to summarize that is a good indication something is wrong.

Overcomes Resistance. One way the patient expresses resistance is to say at the end of each interview, "Well, not much happened today." The practitioner should not let the person get away with that because after awhile the patient begins to believe nothing is happening and becomes hostile. In every session something happens, good or bad, positive or negative, or both, and should be called to the person's attention. No matter how much he has done in an interview, the patient's inclination is to be unaware of what happened. The summary should help the person feel something happened. The patient must go away feeling that whatever happened or did not happen was because of what the therapist and he did. Something would have happened if both had worked more effectively. When the summary indicates the patient did not do enough, his disappointment often serves as a goad to do more the next session.

The therapist should especially summarize every session when the patient begins to improve and the improvement counteracts some of the pleasures the person enjoyed. The patient is losing some of the secondary benefits of her pathology and feels she has a right to be hostile. Therefore, the summary emphasizing the person's progress makes up for what she has lost.

A summary of each interview enables the person to avoid becoming afraid of his confusion. If the patient is confused but resistant to coping with the confusion, the therapist should not summarize. The resulting increased anxiety may motivate him to try to cope with that of which he is afraid.

Integrates. The summary is important as an aid to integration. First, it points out that something did happen which the patient must emotionally accommodate herself to.

Second, it indicates why something did not happen when it might have. The why is a generalized why indicating that patient and therapist have hit some kind of resistance. It is not a specific why because the practitioner really does not know why. In this situation, the person has to live with the awareness there is something about himself he cannot tolerate knowing. It becomes an itch he has to scratch until he can face the intolerable and combine it with the rest of the picture he has of himself. Summarizing lets the patient know what the therapist heard. If the patient is using free association, it is very important that he feels his production is not considered senseless. Even though the associations are very chaotic, they are not as chaotic as the patient thought. The thoughts are saved on the tape and made enough sense so that the therapist could give them back. The therapist organizes the patient's associations and enables the person to see what happened in the session. Clarity about what is happening makes it possible for the patient to form and accept his own interpretation.

Summarizing gives an overview of the session which endows it with a meaning it would not otherwise have. The therapist brings out the pattern underlying the patient's behavior and relates it to one of the case themes. The patient gets lost in the details of the session or forgets them. It lets the person know where she is going in therapy. If the therapist can summarize an interview and both feel they're getting somewhere, there are no problems.

Within a relationship, the patient feels safe enough to tell the therapist about her distorted views of reality. For example, the patient may talk about the unreal suspicions she has of people. The therapist and patient discuss the person's distortions. A distortion is taking a fact and making it mean what one needs to have it mean. Discussing helps to reduce the distortions and the shame the patient feels about them. As the therapist gives the distortions back in a summary, the patient sees them as distinct from herself as a person and is able to either remove or further reduce them.

After the person listens to many summaries, he may eventually find there is an unconscious unitary thread running through them. This continuity gives the patient confidence in the concept of the unconscious. In the beginning of treatment, the unconscious usually means nothing to the person except as a book definition. If the therapist is going to work effectively, the unconscious must have a reality for the patient. What greater significant reality can it have than if the person finds out as he goes along that he is living on a very deep level of which he was not aware? A series of summaries can make tangible the intangible unconscious with which the therapist and patient are working.

Fantasy

Aspects of Fantasy

Every person is a psychologist and/or a philosopher because every person—even those who accept it—is afraid of death. Philosophically, they constantly question the meaning of their lives because they know life leads to death. Psychologically, they give reasons for their behavior and feelings and try to find theories by which to organize them. Without fantasy, they must be psychologists or philosophers to feel their lives have meaning. When people stop being psychologists or philosophers, they lose themselves in fantasies so that life can be as they want it. Their lives have become too meaningless to endure as they are.

Fantasy is the human being's ability to stretch the world of reality so it fits her. An individual finds that reality is confining at best, so she stretches it; she imagines having at a future time what she does not have now. A fantasy is an exploration of the future with the center in the present.

The most important way to get at a patient's problem is to have him reveal his fantasies. This is especially so with character disorders. The encapsulation of any emotional problem causes extreme frustration. The person cannot live out his emotions and feelings because he is unaware of them and hence unable to find a comfortable and satisfying balance between his emotional needs and the demands of reality. His life becomes more and more frustrating. To live in spite of these frustrations he has fantasies. The greater the degree of frustration, the greater the degree of fantasy life. If he reveals his fantasies, the therapist has a good understanding of how, when, and why the patient flies from reality.

The patient and therapist can understand what a fantasy satisfies if they ask, "What does the fantasy say the patient wants or is looking for?" Fantasy always says yes: reality usually says no. In a fantasy the patient is trying to turn a no into a yes. This gives the person and the therapist a clue to the answer. For example, the patient who works at a desk constantly fantasizes working with his hands in an outdoor setting. He entered his present employment because his family got him the job. He could not stand up to his family and say what he really wanted to do.

Life is so short that we cannot possibly have all we wish. It is better for a patient to know what she wants out of life even if she cannot have it all. Without this knowledge, the person feels a vague frustration; she wants something but does not know what it is. If she is aware of what she wants and it is possible and reasonable, she can try to get it. When something is not possible or reasonable, she can make a compromise or an adjustment, that is a part of growing up. Life, with its limits and requirements, kills many of our dreams. Fantasies make life's restrictions tolerable.

Fantasy and Reality. Fantasies make it difficult, sometimes impossible, to deal with reality. Reality can never be as satisfying as a fantasy. Living in a fantasy is very pleasurable; life is as one wants it. Reality, by contrast, is so disappointing that it leaves the patient angry, frustrated, and unwilling to participate.

I cannot define reality, but I have an idea about it. Reality is the way nature uses human beings to perform certain functions. Persons who let nature use them are living naturally and have a chance of getting some of what they want.

Fantasy is unrealized potential. Reality is realized, fulfilled potential. Meaning is the synthesis of fantasy and reality as it is dramatized in life. In their lives, human beings live a certain reality. In their fantasies, patients talk about how they would like to live. The difficulty in matching reality with fantasy comes out of the meaning these persons have attached to their lives. For instance, a married gifted artist has a routine job. She believes her first obligation is to support her family, financially and emotionally. She would feel too much guilt if she abandoned the family. Instead, she tries to make as much time available for painting as she can and fantasizes living a painter's life.

Fantasy as a Contradiction. Talented persons react to their fantasies by doing something with them creatively or artistically. They put fantasies into words as poems or stories, they paint pictures, or they create images in their minds. There is enough satisfaction in expressing the fantasy so they do not need to do anything more about it.

With people who are not artistically endowed, the fantasy is self-destructive because they make it a rigid blueprint of what reality must become. The only way a person can avoid that is to keep fantasies on the level of a rough idea.

The inevitable contradiction is that maturity kills daydreams. A person either stays a child and dreams or grows up, and the dream is killed. Fantasy is a doll that either men or women can play with. As they grow up, they have to stop playing with dolls.

Yet, to live they have to escape from reality into fantasy. If the person fantasizes and loses contact with reality, she will die. It is a question of somehow living with one foot in the world of fantasy and the other in reality. Although therapists cannot do much about the contradiction, remembering it should help them feel less smart than they think they are.

Lying. Lies are not lies, they are fantasies. They are what the person wishes her life was like. A lie is a way to put a fantasy into action. I have a fantasy of being a great swimmer and I do not even know how to swim. If a lot of people were talking about swimming I might say, "You know, I'm going to get myself ready to swim the English Channel." I am not saying I am going to swim it. I am saying I am getting myself ready to do it. I am having a great time saying it. This is implementing a fantasy.

A lie is a distortion or an evasion of what the therapist would say is true. A patient lies to evade or detour around a painful truth. If the practitioner examines the detour she can learn what the person is trying to avoid. The therapist does not have to be specific about the lie because she is dealing with attitudes, not facts. All she needs to know is that the patient is trying to get away from something that is emotionally painful. If the therapist uncovers that attitude she can infer what is going on. Once a patient was describing his childhood that was obviously emotionally deprived. When asked directly what kind of childhood he had, he said it was a happy one. The therapist deduced the patient could not tolerate all the actual pain that existed when the person tried to recall his childhood. Many times, fantasies contain what the patient has wanted since childhood.

Fantasy and Free Association. Fantasy reveals the patient's feelings more effectively than free association. When a patient free associates, that is, just talks about anything that comes to mind, she gives the therapist a lot of irrelevancies as well as significant emotions. A fantasy contains the thoughts within a specific context so the therapist gets important emotions without all the inconsequential associations.

For example, a patient was cruelly dropped by his girlfriend. He denied feeling angry or helpless. He had a fantasy in which the police arrested the girlfriend for prostitution. He was the only one who could get her out of jail and did so, only to walk away from her when she wanted to thank him. In that fantasy he also condemned her because, "like a whore," she had sex with him outside of marriage. If he had not shared the fantasy with me, we would have had to go through a whole gamut of thoughts. It would have been very difficult to relate the associations to the anger and powerlessness he was denying.

Patient's Fantasies

The patient must have a very good relationship and a great deal of confidence in the therapist before the practitioner gets fantasies to work with. The first thing the therapist should do is to find out what the person wants that she cannot get. She may not even know. The practitioner should explain that a fantasy is a story with a beginning, middle, and end that describes what the patient would like reality to be. Fantasies are triggered by internal or external stimuli. Unless the patient is looking for a fantasy, she is not aware she has one. Without the need to reduce emotional pain, the person is either not aware of or not reporting fantasies because that would give her feelings of dissatisfaction.

The therapist explains the need for fantasies and how difficult it is to work without them. This difficulty should not be minimized. A fantasy indicates what the person cannot have in reality and so has to be enjoyed in fantasy. A fantasy is probably a symptom of something in the patient's life having gone wrong, that is, become pathological. Pathological is when what is supposed to function does not work or functions to destroy the person instead of allowing her to live. A fantasy highlights the patient's problem so that both therapist and person can clearly see it. Without fantasies, treatment takes much longer because it is harder to determine the pathology and how it affects the person. Sometimes the patient's problems are not resolved because her behavior is derived from undiscovered fantasies.

The therapist should not work with fantasies if there is a chance the patient's emotions may easily overwhelm him and make him psychotic. Working with fantasies releases much unconscious material that might push the patient into a psychosis. With such a person, it is better to stay on the surface.

Some patients are so lost in fantasy and have so little connection to reality that their fantasies should be left alone. A therapist who dissolves such a person's fantasies has removed the brake that keeps the patient out of psychosis. An example of this is paranoia, based on one or more delusions involving much fantasizing divorced from reality.

Where it is safe, therapists should use every chance to work with fantasies as soon as possible. They should place greater emphasis on fantasies than on dreams, although patients at first see their dreams as more important. The fantasies more effectively reveal and help reduce pathology.

The therapist has to carefully feel his way in deciding how much to tell the person about what a fantasy means. Such explanations might disturb the patient enough to make her stop reporting fantasies. The therapist should start by discussing the fantasy superficially and little by little see how much more understanding the patient can tolerate.

Fantasy as a Reality. The patient's fantasy is the therapist's reality. The therapist helps the patient deal with fantasies as realities by accepting them as givens. When the therapist feels this, the patient feels something similar and talks about the fantasy the same way. To a patient, a fantasy is a strange reality that he cannot tell anybody. As the therapist talks about the fantasy as a reality, the patient gets some distance from it and adopts the therapist's attitude toward the fantasy. Should the patient tell a fantasy containing pathology to someone in the everyday world, he would be considered crazy. Because the therapist examines the fantasy and talks about it as if it were reality, the patient reports more and more fantasies. For the first time, the patient recognizes his fantasies for what they are.

The therapist should not stress the unreality of a fantasy as this makes the patient self-conscious. When the patient reports her fantasies, no matter how bizarre, the therapist should listen and question and discuss them with the person as if talking to a mechanic about fixing a car. Treating the fantasy as a reality makes the patient more comfortable so she feels free to report more fantasies.

Childhood Fantasies. Most therapists tend to look for fantasies about the present or the future. Those fantasies are important, but their importance is based on their foundation in childhood fantasies. The therapist should work with childhood fantasies whenever possible. The practitioner can ask for them when it is appropriate but usually has to wait for an opportunity to do so.

There is a great certainty of finding fantasies in those people unable to let themselves know what they are feeling. It is one of the few ways left for them to feel or do anything. Where the emotions are encapsulated, as in character disorders, the fantasies go back to childhood and not forward to something else. At some point in their lives, as these people matured and met the world, they were stopped by something which is different for different people. Instead of trying to go on or take a detour around the impediment, they went back to their childhood fantasies.

Childhood fantasies are never resolved because they are based on omnipotence. They are contained within the person and become a part of the person. At least two important things are discovered when childhood fantasies are brought out: what the patient really wanted in fantasy as a child, which was probably unobtainable, and how it carries over into later life. If it carries over, the therapist can learn what arrested the adult to such a degree that he had to go back to childhood fantasies. Learning what makes the patient regress makes it possible for patient and therapist to remove the roadblocks that keep the person from growing. Therapists find much of the material needed for continued practical treatment in childhood fantasies. The childhood fantasies are very influential and in many instances explain the patient's current adult behavior. A person whose time and energy are preoccupied with life in the present gives childhood fantasies no outlet to disturb them.

Fantasy as Emotional Pathology. People who are highly disturbed cannot think clearly at all. All they can do is wishful thinking which is fantasy. Unless these persons have some outlet for their disturbances, they express themselves not in what they have, can have, or should have, but in what they wished they had and that is fantasy. Their fantasies blind them to their reality. Concretely this means the person is driving at night without headlights or with a mud-covered windshield that the wipers cannot clear. The therapist's job is to get the headlights working again or clean the windshield.

Every fantasy has a history. When patients fantasize about present situations, whatever resolution they arrive at through fantasy is a result they have arrived at before because in similar past situations the same frustrations were there. Any one fantasy about any aspect of the problem contains a statement of the whole problem.

Asking patients to imagine themselves in certain situations does not uncover the kind of fantasies in which patients manifest their pathology. The manifestation has nothing to do with imagination. The therapist is looking for a compulsive expression of the patient's pathology that has detoured into fantasy. Very often these are fantasies the patient wishes she did not have and tries to forget as soon as she can. I ask the patients what food they dislike. If, for instance, they tell me they do not like liver, I tell them these fantasies they do not want are liver fantasies. They are the ones I particularly need because they tell us a great deal about their problems. There is no general principle for determining if fantasies contain emotional pathology. This is decided on an individual basis with each person.

Frequently, the pathology is expressed sexually. The sexual area develops early in the person's life and is his most secretive part. The patient's pathology usually gets started somewhere in the early developmental years also and the tendency is to connect it to sex. Let us say the patient cannot tolerate being emotionally close to another person, male or female, but at the same time hungers for intimacy. The frustration shows up in sexual fantasies that emphasize emotional warmth instead of lust. The frustration was pathologically detoured into sexual fantasies that prevent the patient from trying to meet his affective needs in reality.

Working with Fantasies

Therapists can be nonjudgmental about fantasies when they know what they are going to do with them, why they are doing it, and if they have some idea of what the ultimate goal is. It is as if a person looks at a hammer and says, "Oh, that's a nice hammer," which is judgmental. If she picks up the hammer and starts banging nails in with it, however, she is too busy using the tool to be judgmental.

Connect Fantasy to Reality. Fantasy is a way of getting around a reality the person cannot handle. A fantasy is effective if it rejects reality as it is but portrays a reality one needs to have. The therapist must explore the patient's reality as it is to understand the reality the patient needs to have. If the therapist talks about the fantasy without relating it to the patient's reality, the discussion becomes a fantasy. Exploring the patient's fantasies increases their number. The patient runs the risk of getting lost in them and trying to realize the fantasies. At some point, the therapist must bring in the reality to which the fantasies are connected otherwise the person reinfects herself even more. The person has to realize her fantasy is a fantasy and not a reality. Fantasy can be used as a seasoning of reality if there is a reality to season. The patient wants to and should use fantasy in relation to reality, not to deny reality. The fantasy is to help the person find new ways of dealing with reality. The therapist relates the fantasy to the reality the person is detouring.

If the therapist does not work with fantasies until she knows what to do with them, the patient will give fantasies to entertain the practitioner and make himself interesting. As a result, the patient injects himself into fantasy. The therapist at the end of the session must summarize what happened that day and what they did with the fantasy. As long as the therapist reports the fantasy and ties it up with reality, she avoids the possibility of the patient becoming lost in fantasy.

The practitioner should constantly explain that by reporting the fantasies the person exposes them; by putting in new factors, they dissipate. Many times an ancient mummy disintegrates when the sarcophagus is opened and air strikes it. The same thing happens to fantasies exposed to open discussion between therapist and patient. Patients tell fantasies to get rid of them. It helps the person to cope with his spouse, children, family, and life in general instead of living in a dream world. When this explanation is not repeated, the patient just tells a fantasy, not knowing what the therapist is going to do with it and becoming more and more embarrassed. The patient is conflicted between wanting to keep the fantasy and wanting to get rid of it. The therapist must make the need to get rid of the fantasy stronger than the desire to keep it by pointing out what becomes possible when the person is no longer attached to it.

The therapist concentrates on what the fantasy does for the patient, not its relationship to the person's pathology. The therapist explains the fantasy step by step. By discussing both positive and negative aspects of the fantasy, the patient feels the therapist understands what the fantasy means to him. The practitioner asks the patient to tell more about the fantasy, all he can remember, and explains what it apparently does for, as well as to, the person. Eventually, the patient learns to understand his fantasies himself, but in the beginning the therapist does the conceptualizing.

Finding the Self-Image. A self-image is a combination of what we think of ourselves and what we think others think of us. For instance, I would be very much ashamed and afraid to have others know whether I have used prostitutes for fear of what they would think of me and because of how I view myself. A person's self-image is a great determinant of her behavior. The way a patient behaves in a fantasy exposes her self-image.

The tendency of patients is to run away from seeing any image of themselves. They enjoy looking at pieces of themselves but cannot tolerate the view of an overall self-image. Patients need to know who they are because then they know what they want and do not want. The way people behave in their fantasies exposes self-image.

The therapist should tell the patient: "Your present state of what we call the self-image is like a lump of sugar thrown into a cup of coffee. Each of your fantasies is a cup of coffee and what is supposed to be you is the lump of sugar dissolved in them. All that is supposed to be you is dissolved in all different kinds of cups of coffee. I need to know your fantasies because that's the way we recover you. From them we can either emerge with some lumps of sugar and know who you are or you'll remain as you are and dissolve into nothing."

How to Work with Fetishes. In one case, the fetish was a long strand of blue silk that my patient gave me. In the interview I asked him to hold one end in his hand, close his eyes, and tell me the things he would imagine if he were to masturbate. It worked on two levels. On one, the fantasy became a reality in the sense that he was not fantasizing by himself but in front of me. The fantasy became a reality because he shared it with another human being. On a second level, he was actually trying to use the fetish with me, but it did not work because he was not masturbating. We both held it and saw that the fetish was nothing but a silk strip. It had lost its power because it was shown to be unable to do anything by itself.

Testing Fantasies. As patients become aware of their fantasies, they begin to strongly realize that they are living in a dream world: that if they live in fantasy they will have to give up actual living in life. Patients then begin to test fantasies by comparing what they get from reality against what they get from fantasy. For instance, the patient with the previously mentioned masturbatory fetish liked the things he could do in fantasy using it. As he began to have sex regularly with his wife, he found that although he missed what he could do in fantasy, he gained in the emotional satisfaction of a closer relationship with her. Eventually the fantasies dissipated.

Dreams

The First Dream

The therapist should tape record all first dreams. They usually contain the essence of the problem although the practitioner may not know it at the time. A few months later, the therapist can go back to the first dream and see the problem and its ramifications.

Using Dreams

I tell the patient that I need the dream, even though I cannot or will not interpret it. We talk impressionistically about the dream in terms of what is happening in the present. I ask the patient for her impression of what the dream is about and then give my impression. These impressions do not have to be in agreement. Therapists use the one that seems most useful for describing what the patient is currently feeling and furthers the uncovering of emotions and feelings. Frequently patients are afraid to give dreams and forget them because they feel therapists will learn too much about them. If therapists reassure patients they cannot know what dreams mean and that their reactions are impressions of what the person is unconsciously feeling, patients are less apt to resist telling their dreams. In this way, therapists can reduce the anxiety which surrounds a revelation of self.

The deeper unconscious aspects of dreams give the therapist an idea of which direction to take. I do not openly discuss these with my patients. I have found that interpreting dreams does not change how patients feel. They gain an intellectual understanding of themselves while the emotional pathology remains.

Many times the patient's dreams reveal what is happening between the patient and the therapist. For example, early in the treatment a patient reported a dream about being in a new classroom as a reaction to being in psychotherapy.

Working with dreams triggers further reactions from the patient's unconscious. Dreams are not sought when therapists believe patients are too shaky to cope with unconscious material. When it is appropriate to work with dreams, their availability greatly helps patients to get well.

Some of the many possible impressions of a dream are right, some wrong. My patients have said, "Gee, that's wonderful, that's right." And I have answered, "If we had more impressions, they would be just as good as this one. They will all sound wonderful, but they may or may not be correct. We don't know." Using dreams impressionistically is tricky. It is an art that depends on the therapist's immediate response and the feel of the patient at that time. The patient can give the therapist a similar dream another time and the impression could be quite different. There is no one way to react.

Dreams are rarely used near the end of treatment. Unless the therapist is careful, the patient may prolong treatment by involving both in the attractions of dreams. If dreams are worked with at all, they are still used in relation to the present reality.

Hiding in Dreams

Sometimes patients bring in dreams as a way to hide. They use up so much of the sessions discussing their dreams that the therapist does not know what is going on emotionally in their everyday lives.

The way I get to patients' everyday lives through their dreams is to say to them, "What we're trying to do is to find out what happened to trigger this dream. The most unimportant thing may have had an effect on the dream. Did you have breakfast this morning?" It is very possible that patients are not interested in their everyday lives; however, if therapists bring their lives in through their dreams, they become interesting because their lives may have meaning.

The Uses of Anger

Anger is not a static state which is how it is conceived and talked about. It is a dynamic group of fused emotions seeking an outlet. When a therapist or patient deals with anger they are dealing with a fire that is already burning. The question is how to put the fire out. Something occurs and a number of emotions are triggered. Persons experience something but do not know what it is. They begin to see what is happening, react to it, and call this composite of emotions anger.

There are many reasons for being angry, depending on the fusion of the experience, the meanings of the experience, and the reactions to the meanings. Although getting hurt in a football game may involve much pain, it is usually accepted as one of the risks of playing. On the other hand, getting hurt in a non-game situation can make the person angry. Fear is frequently an ingredient of this fusion. People are afraid of what can happen if they express how they feel or if it is known they are angry at someone who hurt them. They may feel guilty because they believe they should not be angry at these persons. Their guilt increases their fear because they must see to it that no anger leaks out. In persons who cannot directly and openly react, the anger is detoured and emerges as hostility, a chip on the shoulder, a looking-for-trouble attitude.

Aggression as a Defense

Therapists usually do not see aggression as the mask of an angry defensive patient. Such a person is using the principle that the best defense is to go on the offensive. The theory of aggression says that a person attacks as a way to defend some part of himself or something outside the self to which he is closely related. Aggression is any form of anger the patient uses against the therapist to defend pathological behavior. The patient attacks because he does not want to let the therapist affect him in a way the practitioner thinks is helpful. Aggression is to make the therapist anxious and scare her off.

If the therapist watches how and when the patient goes on the offensive she can learn a lot about the person's problem. The therapist learns from the way the patient attacks and the context in which he attacks what the patient is trying to defend. For example, the patient who says, "Don't criticize me," when the therapist points out he is evasive is someone who cannot tolerate being wrong and defends by putting the practitioner in the wrong. The therapist does not respond to the hostility or anger or whatever it is with her own anger. She gives it a light touch: "Well, all right, if you want to be angry, go ahead, but sooner or later we'll have to see what we can do about your emotional pathology."

In resistance, the patient retreats rather than attacks. This passive form of defense leaves the therapist with no way of telling what the patient is hiding except by guessing. An example of this is the patient who does not talk or withholds information. Resistance is a concentrated effort to retain pathological behavior using the same methods the patient has always used with everybody. The person does not make a distinction between the therapist and other people. The therapist should stir up the patient and bring the resistance out into the open as a form of aggression where the two of them can see what is going on.

Anger Loosens up a Patient

When a person has made up his mind and is frozen, the important thing is to make him angry at whatever he is frozen about. For example, a patient was unable to break away from the ungiving woman he was in love with until he was able to acknowledge and express all the pain and anger he felt and then became ready to write her off.

A therapist who wants to be heard says something when the

patient is angry because then the person's whole emotional structure is loosened. The patient hears what the therapist has to say because she wants to come back at him. She saves everything the practitioner says, every part of it. Her feeling is, "That son of a bitch, I'm going to see if I can get him." She is looking for ammunition.

Shoring Up. Shoring up is like mining: the deeper the miners go, the more they have to reinforce the mine to prevent a cave-in. Emotional shoring up prevents a psychosis. Although the explanation of shoring up is applied here to the expression of aggression, its more general use is in any situation where the revealing of emotions and feelings have created much anxiety and threatens the self. The more the therapist uncovers raw emotions and feelings, the more the accompanying anxiety needs to be contained by conceptualization. Shoring up reduces the patient's anxiety to a level he can live with. The practitioner must accurately judge the extent to which the patient can express traumatic emotions without becoming overwhelmed by anxiety.

Many therapists believe their patients should emote as much as possible. When the person becomes aggressive, both the therapist and the patient are inundated in fear and anger. The therapist should try to get the aggression out into the open while always keeping the concept of shoring up in mind.

The therapist who gets aggression out into the open without meaning creates a destructive personality, someone who frequently and blindly attacks. The patient is involved in chaos when he expresses emotion because he loses his sense of himself and becomes what he is expressing. Meaning is the organization of chaos. It shores up the self by making the anxiety understandable and thereby contained within that understanding. If the aggression is very upsetting, the therapist summarizes it and the organization of the material creates meaning. Shoring up enables the patient to see the significance of what he has expressed as it affects his past, present, and future and for working together with the therapist.

If parents let a child be aggressive, they can often find out what the child wants; then they have to stop her by setting limits. An aggressive patient does not know his limits and may try to sabotage his treatment. The expression of the aggression gives the therapist an idea of how to set limits. For example, the patient who angrily refuses to cooperate with the therapist is told that perhaps he should find another therapist who will work along the lines he wants. Once the patient knows the limits, he learns how to work with the therapist and vice versa. Setting limits reinforces the concepts in which the emotions are contained.

Floating Hostility

In discussing this concept, it is important to distinguish between hate, hostility, and anger. Hate is anger combined with so much fear of a person that one does not dare show anger. All hate-filled people can do is keep their fear, anger, and hate to themselves. Hostility is detoured anger. Hostile people cannot express anger directly at the person, except by attitude; they have chips on their shoulders. They may take their anger out on something or somebody else as a substitute for the person at whom they are angry. Hostility is also expressed through projection. Projection is like a movie film whose images are projected on a screen. Persons who project locate their hostility in somebody else and react as if it were that person's hostility. When persons feel they will lose control over their hate or hostility, they begin having anxiety attacks. Anger is the direct, open expression of one's reaction to a person or situation.

Most patients are hostile to some degree, even before beginning treatment. It affects the people with whom they come in contact. These persons know they have made many enemies but do not understand it is because they are hostile. They do not grasp that their hostility has become an attitude or a philosophy of life they cannot hide. Such patients are searching for something on which to hang their anger.

Hostility leaves persons unaware that their brakes, their controls over their emotions, are faulty. Anyone can trigger these patients' hostility and they compulsively give vent to it. This concept is particularly applicable to patients with character disorders, who are afraid to express emotions and thereby change their anger to hostility or hate. Therapists attempt to adjust the brakes on their patients' emotions so that expression is neither too constricted nor too loose. Then they can cope with their anger in any way they see fit.

In treatment, the hostility begins to float when patients become aware they are angry. It does not make any difference if they know what they are angry about. These persons try to express their anger, but there is so much that it cannot be fully expressed. It is a bottleneck. Floating hostility brings on acting out. Patients feel they cannot talk enough about their anger so they have to do something with it.

Therapists reduce their patients' hatred or hostility by uncovering underlying fears. This frees patients to bring out their anger. Practitioners should enable patients to simply express being angry without looking for a specific, underlying anger because the source may not be any one anger but a whole group of them. It may be something seemingly unimportant; that does not matter. The significance of the patient's anger emerges later. When the person can clearly see both the anger and fear, the floating hostility begins to lessen.

When the opening through which patients discharge their anger is broadened, floating hostility is reduced considerably. The opening is broadened by uniting two approaches: Patients are encouraged to talk about their anger; at the same time, with their therapists' help, they come to understand their anger. The two approaches must come together; I cannot explain how to do it, because I do it intuitively. It is a matter of striking when the iron is hot, when the patients are accessible to both expressing their anger and understanding it.

By keeping the concept of floating hostility in mind, therapists can see and feel it in their patients in a very short time. Their patients are unaware they are angry, yet they manifest anger as hate or hostility because they are afraid to expose it. As the fear is reduced, persons can express their anger; because there is so much anger they cannot convey enough of it as fast as they want. Practitioners must concretize this concept so patients know what they are talking about. One way therapists can do this is by showing patients how they behave or by playing back recordings that embody the hostility. With an understanding of the idea, these persons begin to look for floating hostility themselves. Both therapist and patient can then use the concept more effectively.

Therapists have given their patients a conceptual category to think and feel about. These persons gain an awareness of their floating hostility and with it the realization they have brakes with which to control themselves if they wish. They have become aware of their fear and anger and can now decide what to do with them.

Treat Hostility Seriously

Patients have a great deal of confidence in their hostility because it has worked for them and gotten them places. As a result, they behave in a hostile manner with practitioners. Their hostility is very serious to them and should be so treated by therapists. Practitioners should talk to them about it, "Look B _____ , you come in here and you're hostile. Here's what you do." Therapists should then show patients what they do. If therapists do not respect their hostility, patients become more hostile and do not know why. What they are thinking is, "That bastard. I feel terrible. I want to hit him. He doesn't take me seriously. It is as if I don't exist." The patient's hostility is a very serious matter and the therapist must give it earnest attention. The therapist should say, "I want to point it out to you to make you aware of your hostility so we can deal with it. Unless you control your hostility, it can turn against us and we won't get anywhere. I'm not asking you to stop doing it. I'm asking you to listen to me, to what I'm trying to explain to you. That's all."

Thus, practitioners erode their patients' character armor the only way possible, by making these persons aware of what they are doing. This is done on an intellectual level because patients do not let themselves be affected emotionally. Eventually, when patients are aware, two things out of many may happen. First, they may become uncomfortable and begin to react emotionally by asking themselves, "Why am I behaving like that?" Second, therapists might have to interpret hostility and thereby trigger the underlying angers and fears. When either one of these points occurs, the concept of floating hostility may be applicable.

Omnipotence and its Application

Every child goes through a stage in development in which he believes he is omnipotent. He becomes frightened when he points a finger at you and says, "Bang! You're dead!" and you fall over, pretending you have been killed. A definition of omnipotence is the feeling of being God-like, all-knowing and all-powerful. Omnipotence in children is their way of living with the knowledge of their weakness. They know that if the adults did not take care of them they would die. Yet constant awareness of their need of others, over whom they have no control, makes them too anxious. Hence, the feeling of omnipotence helps them to lessen their anxiety and to live comfortably in their condition. As they grow older and become more competent to cope with their environment, the omnipotence slowly dissipates. Most disturbed people experience so much frustration that to some extent they are motivated by feelings of omnipotence. In adults it is a vestigial emotion, as if they had not outgrown their childhoods.

When a therapist detects omnipotence in adults, the question should be, "Specifically, what is this person afraid of?" The patient's fear has been suppressed for so long that it sort of ferments and exudes a gas, which is anxiety. Therapists cannot answer what their patients are afraid of and try to find out by simplifying the concept of omnipotence so that their patients can understand it.

The description of omnipotence is a framework each patient has to fill in with actual experiences. If therapists explain omnipotence in plain words, they can ask their patients' help in finding what they are looking for. The therapist explains, "This is omnipotence. I feel that somehow it applies to you but I don't know how. We will have to work together. In giving you this idea of omnipotence I expect that it will percolate and eventually bring up memories and thoughts you will share with me."

In applying this theory, the therapist should try to find periods in the patient's life in which she was weak, helpless, and frustrated; in trying to counteract those feelings she felt even more weak and helpless. An example is when she was a child experiencing a strength-sapping disease such as polio. She would have felt weak and helpless and needed to overcome those feelings. She could not surmount them realistically, so she resorted to fantasy which made her feel strong in her mind, while she felt weak in her body. She was dared by a feeling of omnipotence that made her think and behave grandiosely. After she recovered and grew older, either she lived in reality and discarded the omnipotence or that feeling grew and she became a phony. An exploration of that time of helplessness would uncover what feelings of omnipotence are still functioning in the present.

Omnipotence is a concept that can be used with many disturbed patients. In a male, it seems to take the form of Superman. In the female, it seems to take the form of seduction, the Queen of Sheba. An omnipotent adult is hiding a weakness which he fears exposing. Once the therapist can find the specific fear, the anxiety in that area is reduced.

The Omnipotence of Words

Certain people find an outlet in words. They can talk themselves into and out of situations. As long as they are talking, they are all right. They come to therapy for an hour, talk and get off their chests whatever it is, feel good, go away, and nothing changes. With this kind of person, talking is the equivalent of doing. It is as though words are omnipotent: having said it, it is now done. They have fantasies without fantasizing; their words are the fantasies. They are not in enough pain to want to look at their behavior and change. Examining experiences to understand themselves does not mean anything because they feel no need for it. For these persons, their emotional pain also carries the pleasure of feeling omnipotent through words.

While the frequent use of silence might make them stop treatment, it would also show if they can benefit from therapy. Because they have more fun making therapists run in circles and chase after them, therapy may do them more harm than good. There is no way to predict what will take the place of word-omnipotence. This is their way of life, and in spite of the pain, they are having a good time.

Reliving

Reliving is staying in the present while reexperiencing what happened emotionally in the past. Its purpose is to discover what emotions from the past continue to affect the patient's behavior in the present. To do this the patient must be well based in the present or else he gets lost in the past. An example of this is the veteran who relived his wartime experiences and eventually began doing so at inappropriate times and places.

What Makes It Possible

Personal history is usually made up of memories suffused with emotions that trigger actual experiences again. As these three—memory, emotion, and experience—come together, the person can live retrospectively. There is a tendency to remember that which is forgotten because the person has returned to her past.

Even if patients do not really remember actual experiences, certain feelings come up that bother them which they cannot explain. The therapist explores these unexplained feelings because they contain further memories and experiences that will come to the fore. It is almost like paleontology: the therapist digs and finds remains that have a story to tell.

Reliving the Immediate Past

The general scenario is one in which the patient describes an emotional reaction in the past few days which she does not understand or sometimes cannot even name. All she knows is something happened that has left her feeling upset or questioning. As best as she can, she tries to describe what she is feeling now. Then the therapist asks her to describe the incident in which the reaction occurred. Who was there and where were they in relation to the patient? Can the patient see herself in that situation? When the scene is all laid out, the patient replays the experience, watches herself as someone she knows very well and tells the therapist what she sees happening to her.

An example of this is the patient who complained his wife had not prepared his supper last night, leaving him very upset. He did not know what he was overreacting to. When he looked at himself in the scene, he saw his reaction to the unprepared supper signified to him that his wife did not care about him, and this is what made him so angry. This led to the revelation of a long history of feeling uncared for.

Reliving the Long-Gone Past

In some instances, the patient's pathology cannot be reduced until she goes back in her past to particular traumatic scenes, to reexperience them and become aware of what the situations meant to her then. Usually, it is a situation in which she was still ‚a child, understood it as a child and, as a result, misunderstood the situation. Reliving gives the patient the chance to correct the meaning of the past situation which changes the way she feels about it. Other times she needs to relive the trauma to realize she can now cope with it. A trauma is an emotional reaction the person cannot assimilate. It is the equivalent of undigested food. Much of therapy is a preparation to enable the patient to relive her past when necessary.

NOTE

1. *Webster's Third New International Dictionary of the English Language Unabridged* (Springfield, MA: G & C Merriam, 1963), p. 1174.

5

Attitudes

BASIC ATTITUDES

This chapter about attitudes discusses an approach to psychotherapy that is neither systematized nor consistent enough to be called a philosophy. These attitudes that practitioners must have or try to acquire affect how they view and talk with patients and how patients see themselves.

Philosophical and Psychological Attitudes

Therapists must be able to differentiate philosophy and psychology, because they use both kinds of thinking in viewing patients. Philosophy is an attempt to have an organized reaction to the chaos of life that goes beyond life. It refers to ideals and essences which transcend life and for which individuals may be willing to die. Psychology studies how an individual tries to survive within life's chaos and uses its knowledge to keep the person alive. Philosophy talks about how things should or could be. Psychology deals with things as they are. Philosophy is future oriented, preparing a person for how to behave when a situation arises. Psychology is retrospective because it tries to help and understand human beings by looking back at what has happened. Persons who have emotional problems are able to remove or reduce them if they know something about how they got into those difficulties. The therapist/philosopher must understand the general philosophy by which the patient lives. At the same time, the therapist/psychologist attends to the psychological meanings of the individual's experiences that may not coincide with beliefs of that person. A person may believe in helping her fellow human beings but in all of her experiences feel and behave as if she lives in a dog-eat-dog world.

Human Beings Tend towards Health

The tendency of human beings, when they are not emotionally constricted and are free to move in any direction, is toward health. Health is the ability to cope with life in a fulfilling and satisfying way, even when we do not get what we want. I may not have gotten what I wanted, but I can take comfort from having done the best I could. I understand why I could not get it. There is nothing for which I should blame myself.

Flexibility is one of the abilities needed to live healthily. Its opposite, rigidity, equals emotional pathology. Whatever decreases the choices naturally available to a person is pathological. Using Edmund W. Sinnott's concept from *Cell and Psyche, the Biology of Purpose*, health comes from protoplasm, which as it becomes more complexly organized, develops consciousness and goals from within itself.[1] The more protoplasm can accomplish its ends, the healthier the person is, both physically and emotionally.

Because what is good for the patient is determined from within by the patient's protoplasm, it cannot be specifically indicated by the therapist. I do not know what the aim of human protoplasm is. The therapist should try to reduce or get rid of what is harmful in patients, that is, whatever prevents protoplasm from finding adequate direct expression. When patients are helped to not harm themselves, self-understanding and the ability to make beneficial choices may follow.

Through heredity, protoplasm imposes a basic pattern of behavior and feelings on the individual at birth. Consciousness and self-awareness come to the fore as the person matures. They bring with them both the destructive force of anxiety, as the person comes to realize what life can do to a human being and the healing power of self-understanding. Persons enter psychotherapy because an awakened consciousness has looked on their historical design of self-expression and found it inadequate for present use. A different variation of the basic pattern must be designed. As if they were weavers working on their own looms of life, patients try to create variant patterns out of their life experiences to meet present needs. On a high level of awareness, patients throw the shuttle back and forth, from their present to their past and from their past to their present, occasionally getting a glimpse into their future as they try to understand and modify their emotions and behavior patterns. The therapist should remain in the background of this process.

Human Beings Are Open-Ended

This approach sees human beings as open-ended, with no final answers, no final results. Everything is in a process of becoming. At birth, people are endowed with certain abilities and talents. Life may or may not give them the opportunity to express what they have. However, a minimum of talents and abilities must somehow find expression.

People in psychotherapy are those who have not been able to find a satisfactory way to express what they have. These patients have been pregnant all of their lives, but have not given birth. They are still trying to give birth to something. A good therapist is like a good obstetrician; knowing their therapists are facilitating birth, patients try harder. Patients have to know their therapists understand the problem of being pregnant and not giving birth. Eventually, patients try to give birth to something. It may be a feeling, an idea, or a desire. Sometimes patients may never get what they really want. Understanding why they cannot have what they want enables them to live more comfortably with themselves. They are able to accept the limits imposed on them.

All of this is to help human beings to become people, a condition which maximizes the ability of protoplasm to express its aims. By people, I mean those who have fused their particular maleness or femaleness with all the rest of what they are as human beings, without emphasizing their sexuality.

Derivations from Henri Bergson

In *Creative Evolution*, Henri Bergson discussed the human intellect's natural disposition to understand things as a series of static, discontinuous pictures.[2] Therefore, human beings are unable to intellectually comprehend life, especially emotions, which are always in motion. To understand a thing, human beings must merge with and feel as if they are the object. Bergson calls this ability instinct, a sympathy with objects felt rather than thought, that provides an innate knowledge of the thing. He defines intuition as instinct that has become disinterested, self-conscious, and capable of reflecting on its object and enlarging it indefinitely. Knowledge of a patient, therefore, is intuitive, coming from the therapist's emotional immersion in the patient and watching how the process the patient is in makes the therapist feel. Therapists submerge themselves into another person's personality as if they were putting on a coat, noting how it feels to wear the coat, and from those sensations make further inferences about that personality.

I do not accept Bergson's concept of evolution as the way life is used to express an *élan vital*, a force that goes through all forms of life seeking increased consciousness. I am not convinced such a purposeful force exists. Bergson demonstrates its existence by the arguments of induction. I accept his idea, similar to Sinnott's, that life evolves in the direction of increased consciousness. The purpose of that consciousness is unknown to me.

Bergson talks about the present containing all of the past within it and being modified by that past. The ongoing cumulative effect of the past on the present he calls duration. Lengthen or shorten duration and the present is changed. Psychotherapy is a process. Processes take a certain amount of time to achieve a certain result. If the time length of a psychological process is changed, so is its duration, which changes the emotional result.

Derivations from Wilhelm Reich

In *Character Analysis*, Wilhelm Reich saw every person coming to him as encased, to a greater or lesser degree, in character armor.[3] Character armor is a collection of ego-syntonic behaviors or defense mechanisms imposed on character which the person feels are a natural way to behave. They are reactions to those emotions and feelings with which a person cannot cope. In psychotherapy, this resistance needs to be eroded before resistance to uncovering the existing feelings underneath is encountered. The therapist erodes the patient's character armor in the same way that drops of water erode a rock. After the emotional pathology is reduced enough, the patient's natural tendency toward health takes over.

No Foundation

For all of its sophistication, psychology is a branch of knowledge that has both feet solidly planted in midair. It does not know how to describe its basic units. Nobody is clear as to what is an emotion, a feeling, or a thought. Sometimes, the terms *emotion* and *feeling* are used interchangeably. Anyone can, within wide limits, define these basic terms and be just as right in those definitions as anyone else. No one has shown that any theory about the source of emotions is correct. Later in this chapter, I discuss working definitions of *emotion*, *feeling*, and *thought* to facilitate thinking about a person's behavior. These concepts are useful but unproven.

Emphasis on the Conscious Self

This approach is a form of ego psychology. It uses simple division into conscious and unconscious self instead of the Freudian scheme of ego, id, superego. The focus is on the conscious self which corresponds to, but is different from, the Freudian ego. The Freudian ego copes with the demands of an id, a superego, and outer reality so that the human being can survive and experience whatever pleasure is possible. The conscious self copes only with the demands of outer reality and an unconscious self to achieve a satisfying and comfortable expression of protoplasm. An unconscious self exists, but I have no idea what it is. At best, I can discuss some of what it does. Although not Freudian, much of what Sigmund Freud had to say about human behavior is used in this approach. Generally, I have borrowed from any source of information that seemed useful to me.

GENERAL ATTITUDES

The Method

General Approach

The Mind-Body Problem. The unresolved mind-body problem asks what is the exact relationship between body and mind? Opinions holding that mind and body are of a different nature but interact are called interactionistic. Convictions holding that mind and body are two separate substances with no interaction between them are called dualistic. The belief known as psychophysical parallelism posits that mind and body run along in parallel streams without interaction but with parallel influences. That is, anything that influences the mind is reflected by a parallel influence in body, and vice versa. Isomorphism holds that there is a point-for-point correspondence between conscious experience and the physical situation but not an identity. Mind reflects what is out there, but, like a road map, is not identical with it. Another view denies there is a mind-body problem by saying mind and brain are one.

Because the mind-body problem remains unsolved, therapists cannot deal with the causes of an emotional condition. There is no source to go back to and say this effect came from this cause. Unlike the medical person, a therapist cannot go to a malfunctioning organ of the body as a source of the problem. Instead, without dealing with cause, the practitioner tries to eliminate or modify the effect based on what is known about how a symptom or psychological factor affects human beings.

Let us say the patient knows or feels that without any known cause, under certain conditions, she is always angry. Something happens inside that makes the patient angry. If the patient knew the cause, it could be called up to see how it makes the patient angry. A medical person does this when tracing a pain back to a malfunctioning gall bladder or heart and then determining what makes the organ malfunction. Therapists cannot do this.

When a foundation of basic knowledge is laid down on which psychotherapeutic practice can rest, maybe some direct cause and effect relationships can be established.

Another way to state the mind-body problem is to ask how is an emotion equated with a thought? How does a spoken thought from one person become an emotional and physical reaction in another person? Many times patients' emotions are expressed as bodily reactions. They are made sick, tense, or sore as a result of the therapist's attempt to trigger reactions. Nobody knows how that happens.

The thought that releases the particular emotion in a patient is usually a good guess on the therapist's part. When the therapist is trying to affect a circumscribed limited area of a person's emotional make-up, the thought's effect can be foreseen. Generally, therapists use a scattershot of thoughts in treatment because effects are only partially predictable.

A Basic Problem Does Not Exist. A basic problem, physically or emotionally, is a condition that might kill a person. The idea of an emotional basic problem is derived from the belief that a person's upset comes from a specific source, but this is not so. The problem has no specific existence or location in the person for the therapist to go to. The human being and the emotional difficulty are one and the same. Therefore, people have to be treated as wholes, not as representatives of some psychic disorder. The task is to change overall psychic functioning.

Because no basic problem exists, there is no such thing as a neurosis. A neurosis is a collection of abstract symptoms, a model described in a book. A neurosis as a model and the actual person are two different things. The therapist uses ideas out of books about the model of a neurosis to understand the person: in real life she works with a person who behaves neurotically. Similarly, a basic problem is an abstract condition defined in a book, sometimes called a diagnosis or a theory but different from the real-life person. A therapist can get a lot out of a book if he can correctly assimilate what the book has to say, based on his own experience, not the author's.

Cause and effect may be applicable in the physical world, but not in psychotherapy. In therapy, only what happens while the person is experiencing emotions and feelings matters. Patients should be aware of emotions and feelings for as long as they last. The focus is on the functioning of this process not on a basic problem. Therapists going at the patient's pace eliminate consideration of a basic problem because that pace is the rate at which the patient can accept the uncovered emotions and feelings whose awareness modifies psychic functioning.

Human beings are a composite of many little problems comprising the overall problem. The therapist uncovers the emotions and feelings connected with each little problem and patients begin to understand and explain the relationships between the problems. Every little problem tells something about those relationships. When patients describe the relationships between the little problems, they are describing their pathology both to themselves and their therapists. Therapists must help patients find the relationships and modify them.

Even if a basic problem existed, it would be irrelevant because patients would still have to go through the treatment process. Patients have to talk about their troubles, look at them, feel them, relive them, change them into terms they understand now and somehow this brings about a change in psychic functioning.

The idea of a human being having a basic problem encourages the therapist to utilize the approach of a detective. The therapist tries to get his patient to answer questions bolstering the practitioner's deduction. This approach also fosters the attitude of a chess game between the therapist and the patient. The therapist makes a move to validate his thinking. Then the patient makes a move to protect himself from what he perceives as the therapist manipulating him for some unknown purpose. Then the therapist makes a move, and so forth.

The End Is Not in the Beginning. In the most common approach to psychotherapy, the end of treatment is almost in the beginning. The therapist has espoused a theoretical approach that tells her what information is needed to understand the patient and achieve the result called for by the theory. The therapist proceeds to get the predetermined information. Out of the patient's history the therapist creates a pattern, based on the espoused theory she believes explains why the patient behaved as he did.

Even therapists who label themselves eclectic, using anything they think will be helpful to patients, assume that if they can get sufficient data their patients' histories would reveal the human beings. The reality is the therapist can never get enough information to equal anybody. If this were possible, the therapist would be God.

This method sees human problems as the natural result of accumulated detrimental experiences. Human beings generally relate to each other as end results and cannot see the processes in which they are each involved. The therapist must try to see the patient in processes in which behavior can create many effects and an effect can start many behaviors. Put mathematically, the patient is a vector of many emotional experiences.

Preparation. Character therapy is not social casework, psychological counseling, or psychoanalysis. Taking whatever it can use from all of those disciplines, it puts a particular case into a context in which both the therapist and the patient intellectually understand what they are trying to do, why, and how. From the start, the emphasis in this approach is on preparation. Patients are told what their part is, what the therapist's part is, what the two will do together, and how the patient can help the therapist to help him. Preparation separates the surface cases from surgical cases. By seeing how the patients respond to what they are supposed to do, therapists get an accurate measure of just how much self-understanding their patients can tolerate. Interventions trigger both conscious and unconscious emotions to help patients implement what they are trying to do. Patients work on the triggered material within the established context.

Many times, the two of them will not know what they are looking for and will grope, as if they were trying to find their way out of a pitch-black room full of furniture. The therapist has prepared the patient to use interventions that stir emotions inside the person. Both are in the dark, but because the therapist has more experience, she knows what to look for, or how to grope, better than the patient. Something akin to hitting a tennis ball back and forth over the net begins to happen. Piece by piece, the therapist uses what the patient gives to speculate about what is happening. If the person does not agree, he explains why and thereby tells the therapist what is actually happening or that they are both still in the dark. If the patient agrees, the therapist has put the person in a context where he understands the situation and is able to tell the therapist what is going on.

Preparation reduces anxiety in both therapist and patient because they know what to expect. The patient is more willing to trust the therapist because she can sense the practitioner is not anxious. This makes the therapist more effective. The practitioner becomes comfortable with just knowing about the patient in the present and using that information to prepare the patient for their future work together.

Questions. Another emphasis is on always putting patients in such a position that they ask questions. The more questions the better, especially questions the therapist cannot answer. When patients ask questions, they are spontaneously revealing themselves. A patient's question such as, "How long do you think people continue to like each other?" is symptomatic of his or her problem. It gives the therapist something to work with.

Patients remain in treatment in spite of their therapists' not giving answers to their questions because:

1. The patient continues to have a problem.

2. The patient still has questions to ask as a result of encouragement from the therapist.

3. Unanswered or partially answered questions trigger an emotional explosion. As in mining, both therapist and patient then have to shovel out the rubble and see what they have.

Pragmatism. The therapist should use the pragmatic method at all times while doing psychotherapy. Pragmatism asks, how useful is this theory? Useful is meant in two senses: One, how much does it help the practitioner to understand the patient? Two, what happens if this theory is applied to this person? The degree to which it proves helpful to the person determines its use. Helpful here means enabling the person to live a gratifying life in spite of deprivations and frustrations.

To paraphrase William James's essay, "Pragmatism, Lecture 2":[4] The pragmatic method is to try to interpret each notion by tracing its respective practical consequences. What difference would it practically make to anyone if this notion rather than that notion is true? It does not stand for any special result. It is a method only. It appears less as a solution than as program for more work and particularly as an indication of the ways in which existing realities may be changed. Theories thus become instruments, not answers to enigmas in which to rest. The pragmatist turns away from abstractions and insufficiencies, from verbal solutions, from bad a priori reasoning, from fixed principles, closed systems, and pretended absolutes and origins. This attitude enables one to look away from first things, principles, categories, supposed necessities, and to look toward last things, fruits, consequences, facts. The pragmatist clings to facts and concreteness, observes truth at its work in particular cases, and generalizes. Truth becomes a class name for all sorts of definite working values in experience. The true is whatever proves itself to be good in the way of belief, and good, too, for definite assignable reasons.

Purpose of the Method

In character disorders and other severe emotional problems, the childhood omnipotence of words returns, usually in the form of intellectualization. With such words these adults feel they can do almost anything, the way children feel. They live in a world of words that they manipulate. They feel they can control people with words—and many times they do.

The interventions are geared to at least two important purposes: uncovering the person's omnipotent use of words and proving to the patients that words are not omnipotent. Patients find they cannot use words to cope with the reactions triggered by the interventions because words cannot change the emotions and feelings. They learn the limitations of words because they are faced with many interventions and resulting reactions that they go through step by step by step. Patients who respond to this approach are thinking people. Character therapy enables them to think about themselves and begin to feel what they are thinking.

These people have completely meshed words, feelings, emotions, and behavior into one, so that talking is the same as doing. The purpose of this method is to separate words from doing so they are not equated. The omnipotent use of words is decreased so that patients have to deal with words as they are connected to reality; then words and reality become synonymous. The aim is to enable patients to eventually see that words are one thing, behavior is a second thing, and reactions are a third thing. As they are not one, they have to be brought together to mesh in a way comfortable for patients.

Personal History

The mental health field assumes that the parts of a human being's personal history add up to the whole person. This is not true. Personal history does not tell us what persons are actually trying to express, only what they have done, to which any number of meanings may be assigned. People know when they were born but not why they were born. Personal history produces facts, not what the facts mean. Human beings are more than the sum of their historical experiences.

Personal history, unless it is applied to the present, is useless. The uncovering of the past without a specific purpose in the present does not lead anywhere. It may be interesting, but it may be of little other value.

All personal history is distorted because the past is viewed from the present and emotions that operated X number of years ago no longer exist now. Let us say you behaved in a certain way at the age of 20 and look back at it now that you are 40. From the present, the past behavior looks and feels distorted. You wonder how you could have done those things. You feel differently now because your emotions are different. Personal history is an emotionalized myth because anything that you look back on is something that never was the way you see it now.

Many times therapists and patients misuse personal history to rationalize patients' pathological present behavior. They excuse it by saying, "Because this is like a situation you were once in, you can't help behaving now as you did then. Eventually this must change." Eventually never comes. The rationalization is an excuse permitting patients to behave pathologically.

Applying Principles Concretely

Crisis situations and helping patients cope with their basic instincts calls for a direct approach. With basic instincts, the principle of fighting an instinct with an instinct is applied. For example, in a life and death struggle between a man and a woman, where one has a stranglehold on the patient because of sex and cannot free himself, the practitioner should help very directly. The therapist should say, "Look here, if you don't do such and such you'll die. It's a matter of life and death." Then the therapist should let the patient choose what to do. It is not the time for therapists to sit silently and listen. Using the self-preservation instinct to counteract the sexual instinct is a concrete direct application of fighting an instinct with an instinct.

Adaptation

No Cure

Cure, when applied to the human body, means the removal of a difficulty. When applied to the human psyche, where the difficulty has no location, then therapists are dealing with the unconscious which is basically an unknown. They are dealing with emotions that go back to instincts all of which are dynamic. The dynamic moves and cannot stand still; its very existence depends on movement. The psyche is dynamic. It is always working and cannot stop. It is not possible to trace the movement of the psyche because all of it is in constant movement. The only approach to a cure is by bringing about or trying to make a change in psychic dynamics. There would still be movement but in a modified way. An example of modified movement is being able to tolerate more frustration than before treatment. The mechanical viewpoint of cure does not apply here. It is simply a modification of behavior by increasing awareness, which increases one's understanding, which leads in turn to a greater tolerance for frustration.

Patients are not cured. If therapists are successful, they make life more bearable for their patients. That is all therapists can do in most of the situations. The unconscious is like a moving glacier that picks up all kinds of impediments that influence psychic movement. If therapists can remove those impediments, they modify psychic movement. Life is made easier for the patient, and the therapist has done her job. The patient has more freedom, more elbow room to do what he has to do and will do it.

When therapists say they do not know where a case is going, they are saying they should know beforehand how the patient will react, where the patient wants to go. Patients go where they want to go once their dynamics are modified. The direction no one knows. Take, for example, a person who did not allow himself to feel, to actually experience. When he begins to experience, the patient and therapist will see where the person wants to go now because before modification the patient did not know.

I believe there is a will to be sick and a will to be well. The will to be well is the desire of every person to live life and enjoy it, to feel a sense of accomplishment in life. In psychotherapy, it is very important to reactivate the will to be well and strengthen it. The aim of the therapist is to motivate people toward health in spite of no cure. When they are motivated toward health, they look more sharply and much more closely at what is and is not good for them. When motivated toward illness, they do not look and usually react in a harmful way.

In his essay "Analysis, Terminable and Interminable," Sigmund Freud indicated that in a sense therapy never ends because no analysis is or remains complete.[5] It does end in another sense, when people are able to live with and act on whatever they want when they have generally learned to handle emotional difficulties by themselves. In other words, therapy is the beginning of an end, the end being realistic trouble which is a part of life. When patients are healthy and living, they are always in some kind of trouble. The difference is before therapy there was no separation between the trouble and the patient. The patient was the trouble. After therapy, patients have a lot of distance from their trouble so they can see their troubles, sort them out, and deal with them.

Adaptation in Lieu of Cure

Most of us have problems caused by circumstances, environment, other people, and so forth. To be affected, there has to be something in us that these sources can touch. It is as though there is an inclination, a predestination, that a person is born to be whatever he is. This appears to put psychotherapy out of business because there is nothing it can do about one's fate, but there is.

There are modifications of behavior called adaptations. Adaptation is the ability of people to use whatever is available to get what they want out of situations. They have to work around something emotional in them that does not let them go directly for what they want. Adaptation is knowing how to get out of the way of emotional difficulties one cannot cope with; how to bypass those difficulties instead of becoming involved with them.

All of us are born with some defects. These defects can destroy people if left alone, but if handled adequately, they can enable them to live. A person who has an incurable physical condition, diabetes for example, must allow for it or die. If she takes care of it, she lives. Therapists can help patients who cannot change any further to understand their conditions so they can take care of themselves. Therapists are more helpful to their patients when they know their limitations. Patients sense the practitioner's attitude and find it helps them to accept the limitations in their own lives.

Encapsulation and Adaptation

As people go along in life, they try to get away from unresolved fearful experiences by forgetting them. The experiences become encapsulated, as if they were placed in psychic capsules, shut off from all stimulation. The purpose of therapy is to melt those encapsulations at a rate that does not overwhelm the patient with the released emotion and feelings.

An encapsulation is the successful attempt to block out all conscious and unconscious understanding of an emotional problem. It is one of the sources for all kinds of physical symptoms. When the problem is not encapsulated and the patient faces it, there is the possibility of an adaptation. An adaptation involves a conscious realization of the problem and some feeling or understanding of the unconscious mechanism. A therapist who gives the patient a diagnosis has helped the person create an encapsulation. The patient now has a name for the emotional difficulty and feels it cannot affect her any more. She believes it gives her mastery and understanding of the problem.

Therapists need to work the patient through an encapsulation, when possible. This means that the patient reexperiences the desire or desires creating emotional problems now. The more the patient senses and experiences these desires, the more the patient knows what the problem is and becomes ready to adapt to the present reality. The therapist should not tell the patient what the problems are as that makes it an intellectual understanding, changing nothing emotionally. The practitioner must let patients struggle and fret and open up as much as possible whatever they are trying to say, be aware of, or feel. The therapist should try to have the patient tell what the problem is. When the patient cannot be worked through an encapsulation, the therapist's choices are

1. To work in greater depth, trying to uncover more emotions and feelings leading to the patient's desires.
2. To work on the surface and see if any adaptation results.
3. To discharge the patient, telling her, "I have a pretty good idea of what your problem is. To get to it, I would have to work on a pretty deep level. I don't want to do it. If you want it done, find yourself another therapist."

Changing Pain to Suffering

Patients begin psychotherapy because they hurt. In their blind search for relief they further hurt themselves and others. Psychotherapy tries to change the patient's pain to suffering, which is pain suffused with meaning. Suffering patients understand why they hurt. Suffering can make a person compassionate; he has the ability to see, feel, and relieve pain in somebody else. As patients begin to understand what they are hurting about, they accept and adapt to pain as an unavoidable aspect of life. When patients have really gone through the treatment process, it gives them some choice as to how pain uses them and they use pain.

Psychotherapy, in all its forms, is a religion in that it is based on faith and has little or no foundation. Even so, therapists have to deal effectively with pain or they are out of business. The psychiatrist tries to encapsulate pain in medication. Other therapists have to change pain to suffering. Therapists who accept this philosophy must express it in their attitudes, otherwise it means nothing. The patient picks up this attitude and both of them, aware of trying to change pain to suffering, are better able to work and deal with the patient's problems.

Working with the Patient's Reality

Reality is a booming mass of internal and external stimuli clamoring for our attention. It is overwhelming and incomprehensible in its totality. People see only as far as they are aware of their needs. That determines what parts of reality a person tries to understand and control. The situation is analogous to seeing only what a car's headlights reveal in the darkness.

A reality problem is the inability to adapt because the actuality is so inherently difficult. The obstacle is embedded in the human situation. It is easier to say something is a psychological problem when it is a more concrete predicament. That attitude carries the implication that maybe something can be done about it, whereas a concrete reality problem feels like destiny. The therapist should differentiate between the psychological problem and the reality problem.

Emotional Disturbance

Emotionally disturbed people become unrealistic. Their disturbance is a reaction to a situation that does not fit the other parts of reality they know about. They do not know how to bring the parts together. For example, a patient who feels unlikable does not know what to make of friendly people. The person expects to be rejected sooner or later, but the people remain friendly. This creates much anxiety as the patient waits for the axe to fall and cut the relationship. Such a person may end the relationship to relieve himself of the anxiety. When the patient asks the therapist how to understand the situation, that is trying to be realistic.

Unrealistic patients do not know what they need. It is as if they are driving cars with fogged windshields and cannot see where they are going. In the beginning of treatment, before trying to determine a patient's needs, the therapist should reduce the emotional disturbance so the patient has a rough idea of what is real.

Illusions. People try to reshape their reality to what they would like it to be. They are not aware of what they want but unconsciously try to get it by the illusions they create. Illusions are a very intimate part of a person, but the patient is usually wearing somebody else's clothing in that she has adopted someone else's mirage, not her own. Patients cannot cope with another person's vision because they must meet that other person's needs. They can cope with their own dreams if they know what they are. The therapist should help the patient determine whose illusions they live by.

The Patient's Reality

If a person is afraid and does not know why, that fear distorts reality, creating additional anxiety. By looking for where the fear shows up in reality, the therapist can determine what upset the patient at one time and is still operating now. Finding a point of reality on which to focus brings in all the associations and feelings.

An example of this is a woman who feels men are never to be trusted. Because her marriage ended in divorce, the therapist should assume it was hard for her to have a relationship with a man. No matter what she talks about, the therapist should go back to the negative reality of that marriage and clean out the emotional disturbances as a result of the difficulties she had with her husband. After that, the tendency toward health may take over. The therapist's job is to remove pathology, not to cure.

Common Sense

Common sense is rarely considered a factor in the development of emotional disturbance. One form of it is an uncritical acceptance of life. It says all that meets the eye is all there is. Creative and intelligent people use common sense acceptance to buttress their character armor. They suggest to themselves and others that there is no more to them than what appears. Common sense meets the need of people trying to overlook their inherent dynamic differences from each other. The emphasis is on similarities and sameness. Humanity becomes a coral island built by billions of organisms that were once alive but now are all alike and emotionally dead.

Attitudes Toward Psychotherapy

Descriptions of Treatment

Application of Theories. Psychotherapy is the art of using psychological theories pragmatically. The therapist determines what theory or parts of theories apply to the patient. A theory that does not tightly fit a person should be discarded, because theory dictates the therapist's approach. The tighter the fit, the fewer therapeutic approaches to try and the sooner the theory's usefulness is discovered. Ideally, a theory should fit so tight that no other account of the patient is possible.

All theories of human behavior are like myths in that they are all-inclusive explanations of human behavior whose assumptions cannot bear questioning because they are based on a few experiences. Therapists have to accept theories mostly on faith because theories help bring about results.

Rearrange Functioning. Psychotherapy is helping patients rearrange the talents and abilities they were endowed with, as if it were furniture, to live comfortable and satisfying lives in the present. The person can change the arrangement of the furniture, discard some of it, or if patients have forgotten how they once used the furniture, go back to using it that way again.

An emotional problem comes from one of two general sources: (1) something in the existing furniture arrangement has been upset and is being used in the present inappropriately; or (2) recently, something entered into the patient's life that does not fit into the present furniture arrangement. There cannot be anything brand new in the patient's life because whatever emerges is based on the person's endowment and comes through the person's understanding of the past; that is, what he was looking for. It is new only in the sense that it is an ability that has had little or no use up to now. At the time a function enters, the awareness of its newness is minimal. It may look like an old couch that has been reupholstered; time and use show that it is a different ability. What patients can assimilate depends on their past experiences, endowment, and how life permitted them to arrange those two conditions.

Emphasize Emotional Awareness. Psychotherapy is not an intellectual give-and-take with a little room left for the emotions. When patients ask information questions, the therapist should not simply answer them intellectually with the information but also relate it back to why they are in treatment and what the two of them are trying to do. The therapist should keep reminding patients of this at every opportunity. This counteracts their tendency to be unaware of their emotional problems.

Patients know if therapists are helping them. They can see that without therapists talking about cures. This method of treatment enables patients to see progress and helps them to continue working with therapists because they know what they have done in treatment and have yet to do.

Treatment is effective when it is an emotional reeducation. It gets beyond intellectual discussion to the emotional turbulence that may make it necessary for patients to relive emotionally painful scenes from their past. The emotions are all-important. For some time in the beginning, the intellect triggers emotions. An intellectual approach keeps patients at a safe distance from their emotional agitation so it does not overwhelm them.

Patient's Lifestyle

Myths deal with the mysterious and the unknown to which people respond with questions. Myths are the expression of a human need to give meaning, in some way, to what has happened. It is a form of symbolism. Another important aspect of myths is their repetitiousness. For thousands of years, thinking about birth and death has been mythical in that it has contained the same ideas that express the human response to a repetitive mystery.

Because life and death are both mysteries, what happens at the birth of consciousness is that people create their own lifestyles. Lifestyle is a human being's way of living as comfortably as possible in spite of being different from everybody else. The patient cannot build a lifestyle at birth because he lacks experience and strength. He adopts his parent's lifestyle and has it imposed on him. An individual cannot wait until he is old enough to make his own lifestyle because he needs to know now as a child what to think and do. The child is conditioned, caught, and imprisoned because he made the parental lifestyle his own.

In therapy, the person learns to make a distinction between the family lifestyle and his own lifestyle.

Therapists who can help patients to look at themselves are not giving them myths perpetuating the parental lifestyles. Nor are therapists giving them alternate sets of symbols to replace those with which they came into treatment. Therapy becomes effective when the therapist enables the patient to ask, "Where have I gone wrong?" Once people ask this and other questions about themselves and their therapists explore it with them, their own lifestyles emerge. Most of the time, therapists keep quiet and listen.

In psychotherapy, patients are opened up and kept open while the healing takes place by itself. Keeping patients open means having them remember what they already know about themselves. Their tendency is to forget what they learn. The therapist's skill lies in making sure patients do not close up and, at the same time, keeping them open without cutting too deep into the unconscious. Therapists should repeat what patients know about themselves and make it short and simple.

Change starts with the patient imitating the therapist. The change is not intrinsic at first, but eventually becomes something that is the patient's. The therapist's aim is not be a model of behavior but to break up the rigidity of the patient's feeling and thinking by opening her up. When the patient's rigidity is broken up, she has to be something, so for a while she is like the therapist until she reintegrates those pieces. Eventually, patients try to recreate themselves using the broken pieces to form a behavior more in keeping with themselves.

Therapists are not always successful in helping the patients erase the lifestyle they received from their environment. Instead, practitioners try to help persons to be less compulsive about expressing the lifestyles they inherit.

Therapeutic Effectiveness

One criterion of therapeutic effectiveness is the degree to which patients implement what they discuss with their therapists. It means that talking with their therapists has changed the way they feel to such an extent that they had to do something about it. They are no longer the same persons they were when they entered therapy.

If psychotherapy becomes effective, patients take over the treatment. They begin to initiate questions and search for answers. They want their therapists to tell them where to look. They share with the therapist whatever they have found; with the therapists' help, they try to pull it together and make some sense out of it. Psychotherapy enables patients to ask themselves questions and get their own answers. The therapists' answers do not mean much.

Therapy and Divorce

When psychotherapy is successful, the patients often divorce their spouses. These patients chose their spouses out of the needs of their illnesses which are now modified. When husbands and wives have each had successful therapy, divorce may be avoided. In rare instances, untreated spouses may make the necessary changes by themselves so they can live with the patients.

Character Limits Psychotherapy

Patients in psychotherapy are asking for a chance to start over again. They feel if they could live their lives over with what they know now, they would not make the mistakes they did. At some point in their lives, people look back, see the way they have lived, and know where they want to go, but they cannot use that information to change their future. Protoplasm, through heredity, endowed them with certain characters. They are what they are and as a result will repeat those mistakes. This does not refer to the errors they made because of emotional pathology, which can be modified, but to their inherent approaches to life because of their characters.

Character is unchangeable and refers to how persons express what they are biologically endowed with. What they learn after birth is also expressed through character. Uncharacteristic refers to how expression occurs when persons are afraid to be the characters they are. We are all a mixture of character and uncharacteristic behavior. Psychotherapy tries to redirect how the needs of protoplasm are met through a person's character so that uncharacteristic behavior is at a minimum. Character determines how far persons can change emotionally. Psychotherapy addresses the question of how to help patients within the limits of their characters.

Experience is doing something new, finding that a mistake was made, and then doing it again correctly. Whenever something is done again, it is not the same as the original experience. It is the original experience plus newfound knowledge. So it is a different experience and changes every time it is done. Because one cannot have an experience before the experience, life is full of mistakes. Persons may not make the same errors, but they make similar blunders because of the kind of characters they are.

While this nostalgic retrospective view is within, it goes beyond psychology. It is embedded in life because people live in experiences. All therapists can do is examine, explore the patients' experiences, and try to reduce some of their pain. In spite of what therapists say or do not say, patients decide if they want to start over. Maybe patients see they have made too many mistakes and cannot get to where they want; instead, they elect to go on from where they are now.

Therapist's Attitudes

The Psychotherapeutic Relationship. In a psychotherapeutic relationship, the therapist has organized and pragmatically uses psychological knowledge for the benefit of the patient. A lay person may know a great deal and can apply it but not in as sustained and disciplined a way as the professional. Payment is one way the patient rewards the therapist for her skill. It reassures the therapist that the patient likes her.

Even though patients may say they are confused, they usually have a pretty good idea of what they are feeling and why. Therefore, anything that comes from their therapists should be in the form of a question, not a statement, so patients do not feel that their knowledge of themselves is challenged and that they need to defend themselves. When therapists explain something about patients' behavior, it should always be in the form of a question that asks, "Is this so?" Patients need to have the last word.

Patients must never believe their therapists were responsible for what they achieved. It must always be *we*. The patient and the therapist did it together, with the patient getting most of the credit because the person lived through the treatment experience and did what was necessary; otherwise, nothing would have happened.

Therapists should show appreciation whenever patients do something that is difficult. They should say, "You are helping me to help you. I know it's difficult for you, but I don't know what else to do." It gives the patient recognition and encouragement to keep trying.

When therapists let patients know they are dissatisfied with them, therapists are socializing with their patients. It is more like one friend telling off the other friend. Also, most disturbed people have a tendency to welcome the pain the therapist inflicts. When a scolding is necessary, it should be kept to a minimum.

Therapists should not be too analytical; they must leave their patients room enough to experiment. Experimenting is trying things out, gaining experience. Without enough experience, patients are not ready to talk about what they are going to do. Before making difficult-to-counteract decisions based on their experiences, patients should thoroughly discuss them with their therapists.

Conviction. The basis of psychotherapy is faith, beginning with the therapist's belief in theories whose tenets are unproven. The therapist has faith in her therapeutic ability because she believes that what happens with a patient is a result of her treatment. This may or may not be so. There are still many unanswered questions about what helps a person to change. Patients come to believe what their therapists believe. They reexamine their lives because they have faith in their therapists, who point out their emotional problems to them. If therapists have doubts about themselves or doubts that their patients have psychological problems, patients feel it and do not change emotionally. Therapists must try not to impose the convictions of their faith on patients, no matter how strongly they believe in it.

Trust Intuition. With every patient there are times when therapists must juggle many factors at a time. When they know what they are doing, therapists do not juggle but simply react to the whole person. Therapists juggle when they are responding to only parts of a person. They should go into their interviews and see what happens without any predetermined goals. Life unfolds from moment to moment, day to day. Therapists must remain open to respond to that process of action and reaction; it tells them what they need to know about their patients. Therapists must have faith in spontaneity and intuition. I have said to patients, "Look, I'm saying this to you, but I don't know why. Maybe next time I'll know. Maybe I won't." I react, and patients respect that. So much in psychotherapy is not known scientifically that therapists must have as many approaches as possible. While they do not have to juggle, therapists must know when to react spontaneously.

Sometimes an intervention does not work and the therapist thinks of something else to try right then and there in the session. That does not mean that the new approach will work. As long as the therapist is with the patient, he has to relate to the person therapeutically and trust his intuition.

An important source of the therapist's ideas is what interaction with the patient triggers during a session. When the patient leaves, the ideas should be written down right away, before they are forgotten, and used another time. Such ideas are a response to a live situation and can be very effective. Books and other outside sources teach the therapist very little. A good teacher teaches therapists how to learn from themselves.

When therapists become masters of their art, they have created for themselves what I call psychic radar. Therapists know the patient without having all the facts or information because:

1. They know where to look.
2. They know how to use what they know.
3. They know how to ask questions to get what they have not found yet.
4. They elicit the respect of the other person so that he helps in his own treatment.

Recognize the Dramatic. A drop of water seen under a microscope is its own universe. It contains all kinds of life. All kinds of matter exist in many different relationships. At the same time, a drop of water is part of a river, part of an ocean, part of many other universes. We cannot live without water, and therapists should see the drop of water as symbolic of life itself. This drop is analogous to the moments in a person's life. People live in the *now*, from moment to moment. Every moment is an entity unto itself. All the *nows*, with all their internal and external relationships, equal a life. Patients always feel the *now*, the moment in which they exist. For example, fear is important to patients with much anxiety. All such a patient has on her mind during an interview is the fear coming out of her anxiety. Every particular fear that the patient experiences is important to the therapist because it is important to the patient. What the two of them deal with evolves from minute to minute out of the patient's fear.

Therapists must learn to deal with *now* as symbolic of a person's life. Instead, some practitioners apply all the ideas and theories they have about the way human beings behave. This creates a synthetic personality that never existed and never will. Experiencing anxiety produces fears in the patient that are dramatic to the therapist because she sees where those reactions fit in with the rest of the patient's life. The dramatic affects the person either physically or emotionally, no matter how small the item. It is usually dramatic only to the therapist because she sees its relationship to the whole context in which the patient lives.

Patients' Dramatics. Therapists must realize that when patients are being dramatic they are trying to give some meaning to their lives in an organized form. People whose lives lack meaning may have feelings of depression and futility. Meaning is the difference between sound and music. Sound is just noise; music is organized sound. Everybody's life, physically and psychologically, just goes on; however, there are different ways of going on. When life goes on by force of habit, there is no meaning. A life that goes on with meaning has some organization. When people dramatize, they are playwrights. They compress years into a few hours, as in a play, edit out the nonessential elements, and organize what is left into a drama.

The Self

Known by Opposition

The self is protoplasm that is aware it is a conscious, individual being. Although the self-images the self creates tell us what it does, the self is an unknown. As an entity, it is more a meta-physical concept than psychological. It is an attempt to establish a first principle of cognizant being and to explain human behavior.

People need opposition to feel and be more aware of themselves. They can only know themselves when they approach their limits. The more success in a person's life, the more she needs failure to be aware of herself. A human being is more of a something when she is in a crisis, be she Catholic, Jew, or Muslim. She falls back on the bedrock of herself. When there are many failures, the awareness of self decreases, because then the focus is on trying to cope with an outside environment.

Contentment Reveals the Self. Contentment is a condition of surfeit. People have had enough; they have reached their limit. Happiness has a feverish quality about it. Happy people may feel as if they are whirling around and not quite in touch with their surroundings. It never lasts long enough. The effect fades and it takes more to get back to the same state of bliss. Most people confuse happiness and contentment. They do not realize they are not going to find the continual state of happiness they are looking for. If they realized, they might settle for contentment. In happiness the self remains unknown because there is no limit. In contentment the person says, "I don't want to go any further." The self has emerged through opposition.

Psychological Strength. Psychological strength is the ability to tolerate pain so that people can be what they are. Somehow these human beings survived many crises because they needed to, wanted to, and because they got somewhere. Strength can be defined as reaching for a goal, regardless of difficult people and situations.

The Distorted Self-Image

Therapists must find out what kind of images the patients have of themselves. Who or what do they think they are? The self-image greatly influences the patient's behavior and needs. Usually these patients have distorted self-images, that is, many images of themselves that are not real. An example is the married man who dates women as if he were single.

The therapist's job is to correct the self-image. If practitioners can do that, patients accept themselves as they are and their whole situation changes. Therapists treat people who know a great deal about themselves because they continually polish their self-images to make themselves look as good as possible to themselves. Therapists know where the blemishes are. When the time is right, the therapist tells the patient what he does not want to know about his self-image. The person seems to gain some distance from past and present self-images and briefly sees himself realistically.

Role Playing. Being male or female suggests that not only are people what their characters are, but they play roles as well. Role playing in any situation is a mixture of being the kind of man or woman others expect them to be and being the kind they expect themselves to be. They are what they are—a composite of all the different relationships, expectations, and experiences they have ever had. In the composite is a nucleus, the extent to which a person can answer the question, "Who are you?"

Measuring Progress in Therapy

Emotional disturbance tends to separate the self into pieces. Progress in therapy is the degree to which the self is able to organize in relation to the world around it. An example is the patient having difficulty using an intervention and saying to the therapist, "I can't do this." The "I" is an organization of the self's fragmented pieces in relation to the therapist. Progress is the person's ability to organize and not go to pieces when the world wants something of her. The therapist and patient need this yardstick of achievement so the therapist can indicate progress to the patient who needs encouragement to continue in therapy.

Identity

An identity is an individual self. In identifying with something, an individual self chooses to associate itself with another individual, group, or cause. Some of the elements that define an identity are acquired from *identifying with*. Positively identifying with is a voluntary assimilation from other selves by the self. Negatively identifying with is a superimposition of other selves on the self. In a general way, this means emotional health is equated with assimilation while emotional disturbance is equated with superimposition. The self can emerge only as the super-impositions are divested. In one instance, the self has enough room to breathe; in the other it is suffocating, choking to death, and has to use any means available to survive. Those survival means are the symptoms of emotional illness. Given the opportunity, the self emerges and assimilates. The healthy self has a protean quality that—no matter how much it is modified—always remains itself, whereas the sick self stays within the limits superimposed by the negative identification. The sick self is most alienated from itself in character disordered patients. As it crosses the boundary line into psychosis, the alienation takes on the most distorted and monstrous forms.

The Therapeutic Use of Identity. The concept of identity, as a person's acceptance or rejection of her attachments to the past, to people, and different relationships, is used therapeutically when considered in relation to that person's emotional needs. What does she need and how do her identifications help or hinder her in getting it? A person's identity does not come through her history as it is taken fact by fact but as the patient reveals the pressures she feels, what bothers her. There are very important words, ideas, concepts, in any language that release many associations, feelings, and emotions. Words such as *mother* and *father* may trigger all kinds of disturbances, acceptances, or the need to reject.

Identity implies specific attachments. For example, you may have had the experience of waking up in a strange place in the middle of the night and the only way you know you are you is by recognizing something that belongs to you—a watch, a shirt. Many times patients are in conflict, unable to form a specific attachment, until the therapist helps them to resolve the discord.

Adolescence and Identity. One reason identity is so important is that people have to have some idea of who they are and where they are going because there are so many changes going on in their lives. This is especially applicable to adolescents who feel they have real problems because they are in the midst of both physical and emotional changes. While identity is a problem for everybody, it is a matter of gradation. Adults have asserted themselves within wide limitations. Their need for identity is not as urgent or on the surface as it is with adolescents. Identity is

harder to achieve and much more important to adolescents because they lack life experience, are dependent on their parents,
can only partially assert themselves, and yet want to begin living
their own lifestyles.

Feeling Sorry for Oneself

Feeling sorry for oneself is looking introspectively within and
feeling strongly life could have been otherwise if something else
beyond one's control had happened. It is feeling one made a
mistake but blaming everything except oneself for the mistake.

Neurosis and Psychosis

Neurosis, Psychosis, and Fainting

Neurosis, psychosis, and fainting are three different ways a
human being stays alive when life becomes too stressful. In neurosis, the person's ability to live a satisfying and comfortable life
is curtailed by anxiety. The person becomes an eight-cylinder
car running on only four cylinders. She has limited the degree
of her living by avoiding those parts of her life that frighten her.
In psychosis, the emotions are so overwhelming the person feels
he is on the verge of being entirely destroyed. All of his resources
are geared to contending with emotions to such an extent that
he can barely maintain contact with the world around him. A
person faints when he is exposed to severe difficulties or pains
that exceed the coping mechanisms of psychosis and neurosis.
The person would die right then and there if he did not faint.
Fainting is similar to a fuse blowing out or circuit breaker opening so the house does not catch fire because the circuits are
overloaded.

A neurotic is a person who cannot react openly and directly
in the present situation and detours his emotions. He does not
learn anything from the present because his behavior is a continuing reaction to his past.

A psychosis, or acting out which is near a psychosis, is an
inundation of emotion to such an extent that the person has to
go into unreality to escape destruction of the self. She does not
know what to do or where to go to get relief. The psychosis or

acting out is an outlet for what the person has always wanted to do but managed to control up to now.

Psychosis and Abstraction

The psychotic lives in a world of reifications: she treats abstract ideas as if they were concrete realities. The neurotic also reifies but retains much more contact with reality. When neurotics cross the line and everything becomes abstract, they are in a psychosis.

People who believe they are not whole and who split themselves, for example, into child and adult parts are reifying. Their hold on reality is greatly weakened because they have created abstractions they are treating as realities. Their thinking moves from the abstract idea of being a child to the abstract idea of being an adult, creating a total abstraction. Such people try to cope with realities that do not exist. They have abstracted an explanation of behavior from reality which has no concrete existence and eventually they may abstract themselves into psychosis. Therapists should not use terms that divide the psychotic person, such as "the childlike or child part of you." Practitioners should call on the actual experiences of childhood instead. Those experiences tie the person closely to reality and are more meaningful.

The self is the central authority of the personality as the federal government in Washington, D.C., is of the United States. Although each has its own sovereignty, every state depends on the central authority of the federal government for many final decisions. The awareness of self is very important because if that is lost, a civil war ensues between the parts of the personality, and it can end up in psychosis. The personality must not be divided so that one part struggles against the other to the extent that the authority of the self is lost. If that happens, there is no telling when the parts will turn against each other so much that the person gets confused and loses touch with reality. Once patients divide themselves, there is nothing to stop them from further divisions. That is what psychotics do.

Psychotherapy is based on abstractions; therapists must also try very hard to bring out the reality of the abstraction. For example, if the therapist gives the patient an interpretation, it should correspond to experiences that the patient has had. Patients should feel such interpretations through their experience. These interpretations should be tied to their reality in the same way that their identity is tied back to spouses, children, and past experiences.

Coping with Psychosis

Psychosis is not curable. If life is given a chance to take over, its innate tendency toward health helps the person to get better. Sometimes it is enough if patients are in environments where they feel protected and are given tranquilizers. A protected environment does not necessarily mean hospitalization. It can be created by the therapist as a result of the very close relationship he has with the patient, with or without the use of tranquilizers. Contact with the therapist both by telephone and frequent in-person interviews helps the patient to cope with the inundation of emotion he is experiencing. A patient must feel the therapist is with him, or available as the need arises. Ideally, the patient should be as tied to the therapist as a drowning man is to a life preserver. Even when the psychotic person talks gibberish or is irrational, the therapist understands; the patient understands that the practitioner understands. The therapist is the patient's tie to reality. The kind of protected environment to use is determined by how close a relationship the therapist has with the patient and the degree to which the person is a danger to himself or others.

Theory and Theme

Theory tries to explain why patients behave as they do. This is different from the theme of a case which addresses how the patient behaves. For example, a patient may be unable to tolerate intimate contacts because she had painful familial relationships while growing up; this would be the theory. The theme would be how that person avoids close relationships to escape pain and survive. Therapy cost and time can be greatly reduced when attention is paid to the theme.

Every case must have a theme and a theory, and unless the therapist finds them she is absolutely lost. She will not know what to concentrate on and will never know when she is through. It takes time to find the themes and theories.

A patient's behavior may include many minor themes. The therapist finds the themes, and the patient supplies the music or behavior that illustrates the themes. If the patient understands what material is needed she somehow finds it. The therapist has to explain this need in many ways for a long time before the patient helps. The therapist must also work on the basis of a theory because she has to have some hypothesis from which to work. Experience shows how to correct or throw away the theory and come up with other theories as the case develops.

The therapist should not just tell the patient his theory about the person's behavior. A theory needs verification. The material the patient gives to the therapist should validate the theory. As the theory is revealed, it has to pull together and organize what the patient told the therapist. If the therapist explores the material the patient gives, the person will possibly uncover the theory herself. The therapist should not tell the patient how the material fits the theory. It is the same as saying, "I'm right, you're wrong." The patient then wants to prove the therapist wrong.

Apply Theories to Individuals

Theories are composite generalizations of people and not about individual people as they are. Thus, they are abstracted from a mass of experiences with many people. Because theories are composites, they are complicated. Therapists must simplify the complicated theory and use only those parts that fit the patient.

The therapist works with people to apply ideas. When the practitioner uses a theory, the patient becomes an idea of a person, not the actual person. The challenge is to keep the patient a real person instead of an idea. Patients can sense when their therapists feel they are ideas and resent it bitterly. The therapist should separate herself from her idea of the person, face her patient, and say to herself, "This is a human being. What do I do?"

Emotion, Feeling, and Thought

Emotion is the initial reaction to a stimulus that motivates human beings to draw on their energy for responses. It is analogous to the spark in the combustion chamber that explodes the fuel, creating the energy to turn over an engine. The person churns inside and may have thoughts such as, "Give up. I'm frozen. I'm going to pieces. I'm torn apart." The individual and the emotion are one.

Feeling is the ability of a person to gain some distance from her emotions and put into words what has happened to her. Some time after a stimulus the person stops and says to herself, "Now why am I doing this? I'm acting like a crazy person. What's going on here? Should I be upset?" She wonders, "What's the connection between what was said and my being so upset? I was called a cheat. Why? I'm okay. They're mistaken. There must be some reason. Maybe I did something. Let's try to find out what." By now the person is just a little bit removed from the reaction. She is not the emotion. She is thinking about it. There is a separation between the individual and the experience.

Thought is the synthesis of emotion and feeling. Along with feeling, thought further organizes the emotion and the person so he is able to consider what he wants to do. The thoughts look for a possible way to express the emotion. The time it takes to go from an emotion to the ability to think about it is affected by a number of variables. It can happen in a short time, or it may take weeks. Thought also occurs when a similar situation or person turns up and the individual compares it to earlier experiences. I do not know what causes a person to be totally immersed in an emotion at one point, and at a later point separate herself from the emotion and see it as something within her that she can cope with.

When therapists deal with emotion, feeling, and thought, they have to use an experience to demonstrate the differences between them. Patients tell what they did and therapists help them recognize what is affecting them.

For example, a patient is with her boyfriend, who she thinks has something up his sleeve. She dislikes the way he is behaving but does not know why. At this point she is experiencing an emotion. She thinks he is up to no good. When she begins to think accusingly she is changing an emotion to a feeling. She feels guilty because she is thinking badly of him and angry because he seems to be trying to take advantage of her. The therapist analyzes the situation and points out, if possible, how she seems to have arrived at those feelings. She can see if this is so because she went through the experience. Thought starts as she begins to think about the feelings and decides what to do about them.

Emotions, feelings, and thoughts work with the body to enable people to express themselves; this natural process is found in all human beings. A perversion is a detoured expression of an emotion; something keeps it from manifesting itself openly and directly. Therapists are most interested in removing the detour so that the emotion can take its natural course, through feeling to thought to expression. When the emotion has to go by roundabout ways and come out as something else, it becomes perverted. An example of this is the married couple who must first quarrel before they can feel close to each other.

Bringing out Emotion, Feeling, and Thought

Many therapists ask patients, "Can you share your feeling with me?" That question starts a thought process, which impedes the patient's expression of the emotion itself. When patients share how they feel, they talk about the feeling but do not experience it. They talk about being angry without being angry. The question rejects the emotion and thereby stops the feeling and thought that goes with it. The question should be, "What occurs to you about being angry? Have you been angry at people in similar circumstances? What comes to your mind?"

When therapists ask, "What's going on inside?" they are listening to the patient intently as if it is very important to them. They may be giving the situation a significance in the patient's eyes which does not belong to it. Therapists should try to uncover the emotion and feeling only when there is a great deal of unresolved conflict.

Separating Feeling from Emotion. I once asked a patient, "Why are you crying?" She tried but really could not tell me. She talked a little bit about it: "I cry when I feel like a little girl and when I feel I'm wrong. If I cry and if I'm a little girl, people won't hurt me." I asked her to choose the age at which she was a little girl. When she chose the age of eight, she had a focus for her little-girl feelings. Then I said, "Be eight. What occurs to you? Pick out anything that happened then that means something to you. Where did you live at the age of eight?" I picked out an object she remembered and asked what occurred to her about it. Relating to an object helped her to know what she was then. Feeling like an eight-year-old girl who had done something wrong, she realized her present fear of being ridiculed as she had been then was making her cry.

Feeling as a Risk for Adolescents

We live in a world so unpredictable that to feel means to be secure enough to let yourself go, tumble into an unknown experience, and believe in your ability to land on your feet. You let yourself become aware you are immersed in an emotion, and you trust that something in you will enable you to gain some distance and decide what you want to do about it. Taking a chance like that is risky; how do you know that you are not going to break your neck as you tumble into the unknown? Yet you have to take that gamble to live and be the kind of person you are.

This is not as possible for adolescents. Many times thinking is their substitute for feeling, because they lack confidence in their ability to cope with their emotions. Until recently they depended on other people to do their thinking for them. They fear they may be overwhelmed by their feelings and lose control of themselves. They often run away from feelings, even though it would be better if they could let themselves feel.

Emotions and Thoughts

Emotions and thoughts need each other. They are part of the natural sequence transforming emotions to expressions. They go together like husband and wife. Disturbed persons do not like this marriage and try to get a divorce, so they can live entirely by emotion or entirely by thoughts. Either they lose themselves in emotions so as to be unaware of what they are feeling and thinking, or they stifle knowledge of emotion by keeping themselves lost in thought. This leaves emotions and thoughts disconnected and looking for each other. These people are unaware they made such a split and wind up looking for something they feel is missing but do not know they discarded.

This is not a description of an actual reality but one way to think about emotions, feelings, and thoughts. The concept is that emotion is in search of thought or thought is in search of emotion because as displaced parts of a sequence, they need each other. Persons who separate emotions from thoughts are torn apart and do not know why. They may go into depression or resort to fantasy.

Emotion or thought without the other makes life meaningless. The disconnection of thought and emotion is part of the reason for depression. By finding the thoughts that belong with the emotions, or vice versa, therapists reduce or remove the depression.

Thoughts without emotions are much more effective in setting goals. They go directly to the objective, without taking into account another person's pain, sorrow, fear, or any other effect the aim may have. Thought alone makes life vicious. Emotion and feelings are like a rider not allowing the horse to go wild. They remind people who do something based solely on thought that afterward they will be self-conscious, fearful, and worried about what other people will think.

The character therapy approach tries to bring about change by bringing together emotion and thought. The interventions do that by triggering an emotion leading to a thought. Patients, on the other hand, usually begin with thinking and cannot get back to the emotion.

Therapists work with compulsive, self-destructive behavior. People who do something self-destructive do not know how to do something self-constructive. The pressure of their emotions mandates they must do something, so they do anything that occurs to them. Self-destructive behavior is basically a detour to relieve the pressure of emotion seeking expression. It is an emotion seeking expression without its thought, or vice versa. Such people are cut in two by the pressure to express an emotion. Either they cannot accept the thought that would accompany an emotion or cannot accept the emotion behind a thought. An example of this is the man who emphasizes how tough and masculine he is because he cannot accept his sensitivity, which he equates with effeminacy. Usually, the emotion and the thought are found in two unexpected places.

People involved in self-destructive behavior are upset because they are either operating entirely on emotions or entirely on thoughts, only one half of what they need to use. They may shift from one to the other not knowing how, when, or why because they have no control over themselves. Patients who know their therapists know they have disconnected emotions and thoughts may start looking at how to join them, how they are not joined (which is just as important), or why they are not joined.

One implication of the relationship between thought and emotion is that the therapist should put into words what the patient is experiencing but cannot talk about. The therapist captures the emotion within the words and validates for the patient what is happening emotionally. Despite the general belief that words come first and feelings later, this approach says words and feelings come at the same time. If the therapist provides the words, the patient provides the feelings to go with them.

Emotions and Ideas

If chaos is a bunch of random musical notes and emotion is a rhythm, then ideas are the organization of the notes to that rhythm, making music. Thinking embraces chaos partially, while emotion absorbs it all intuitively. Emotions erase ideas. People who are very emotionally involved do not understand their situation; they simply react.

An idea is a number of related thoughts—a plan, a format— that the human mind forms about a situation. It is the order that the mind imposes on life, which is chaotic. Without ideas, human beings cannot understand the chaos or try to control life.

With an idea, the intellect cuts up reality into pieces. The intellect takes certain aspects of reality and tries to organize just those pieces into a whole, leaving out the other parts. Not only does it leave pieces out, but the intellect also thinks of reality as a collection of pieces when reality is really a seamless whole. Therefore, an idea creates a reality that does not exist.

Therapists have to get back to the actuality from which the artificial reality was concocted to correct the person's ideas. An example of an artificial reality is the belief that it is always best to express one's anger. The reality is that a person has to know when and how to do it. Human beings are conditioned by their ideas of an artificial reality, and therapists recognize when patients are in trouble because their artificial reality does not work the way these persons think it should.

Many people who enter psychotherapy have tried to control all of life through ideas. This is the hallmark of people suffering from character disorders. These people have tried to base their chaotic lives on thoughts. With their therapists, these patients look at their chaos and try to find a meaning involving their emotions as well.

As an example, pain is meaningful if it has a goal. Your doctor tells you, "This is going to hurt." You want to be cured, so you bear the pain. But if the doctor does not tell you anything, and it hurts and you do not know why, the pain seems purposeless and is very difficult to bear.

When therapists work with people, they deal with abstract ideas. People are what they think they are and what others think they are. These ideas change with age, with how a person is feeling, and so forth. I am different now from the person I was 20 years ago. Psychotherapy works with ideas and tries to put them together with emotion. The aim of psychotherapy is the smooth transition from emotion to thought.

When therapists work with ideas, they are always taking chances because ideas are as fragile as spider webs. There is no certainty in psychotherapy. Any pattern of wants or behavior that the therapist discovers and works with will change. Even though people tend to repeat themselves, especially when they are unsure of themselves, the therapist does not know when that repetitive pattern will break down. All their lives therapists cope with uncertainties. As their skills increase they deal more and more with uncertainties, and in the future their skills will lead them into areas they dare not go into now.

NOTES

1. Edmund W. Sinnott, *Cell and Psyche, The Biology of Purpose* (New York: Harper Brothers, 1961).

2. Henri Bergson, *Creative Evolution*, Arthur Mitchell, trans., The Modern Library (New York: Random House, 1944).

3. Wilhelm Reich, *Character Analysis*, 3d enlarged ed., Theodore P.

Wolfe, trans., The Noonday Press (New York: Farrar, Straus and Giroux, 1969).

4. William James, *Pragmatism and Other Essays* (New York: Washington Square Press, 1963).

5. Sigmund Freud, "Analysis, Terminable and Interminable," in *Collected Papers*, Vol. 5 (New York: Basic Books, 1959), 316–57.

6

Treatment Constants

In this chapter, I discuss some of the problems therapists must cope with, no matter what their patients have achieved in therapy. They are the situations that show up in every treatment. Some are grouped under *The Beginning of Psychotherapy*, as this is where they are first encountered, but they can also appear at any time thereafter.

THE BEGINNING OF PSYCHOTHERAPY

This section contains additional comments about starting psychotherapy. In the beginning, patients are intellectually prepared for therapy and achieve distance from their problems. Whenever possible therapists should ask, "What are you coming here for?" and have patients answer the question. The answers give therapists clues for reinforcing the preparation for therapy. Some patients may practice deception to avoid dealing with their problems by deliberately giving different reasons from those originally agreed on. This also gives the therapist an idea of what is going on.

The Beginning and End of Therapy

Therapy starts as a necessity, because anxiety forces the patient to seek relief. The patient should start by asking questions. Treatment becomes a choice when the pressure of problems is temporarily relieved and the patient decides to do something about whatever caused the anxiety. Therapy ends with the ability to make choices and implement them, which keeps anxiety to a minimum because the person feels she has some control over her life.

Duration

Our responses to life are often unorganized and go off in all directions. When we look back, our lives appear anarchic. The therapist organizes the patient's chaotic responses in a time sequence called duration, which is different from clock time. The therapist puts the patient in a context where his life is viewed as one experience flowing into and influencing the next experience. All of his experiences come out of each other and form an organized whole. The emotions associated with each experience measure the subjective length of time at that point in his life. An intensely felt experience seems to last forever; one in which we become so interested that we forget ourselves feels like a brief interlude. Duration is used in therapy because human beings exist in both time and memories suffused with emotions, and this is the only way to sum up how they lived their lives.

Pure duration is the form which the succession of our conscious states assumes when our ego lets itself *live*, when it refrains from separating its present state from its former states. For this purpose it need not be entirely absorbed in the passing sensation or idea; for then, on the contrary, it would no longer endure. Nor need it forget its former states: it is enough that in recalling these states it does not set them alongside its actual state as one point alongside another, but forms both the past and the present states into an organic whole as happens when we recall the notes of a tune, melting, so to speak, into each other.[1]

When a person uses silence and associates in the presence of another person he frequently feels foolish and stupid. If he thought of associating as music and memories as its notes, he would have the concept of *inner duration* to explain and dignify what he is doing.

Inner duration is the continuous life of a memory which prolongs the past into the present, whether the present distinctly contains the ever growing image of the past, or whether, by its continual changing of quality, it attests rather the increasingly heavy burden dragged along behind one the older one grows. Without that survival of the past in the present there would be no duration, but only instantaneity.[2]

Psychologizing

Some therapists simply tell their patients the psychological principles that explain personal behavior. When that goes on long enough, patients become half-assed psychologists, which they should not be. An action resulting from the environmental pressures experienced in a person's context is one thing. It can be studied and its own unique meaning inferred. A psychological explanation is an abstraction outside of the environment and context of the occurrence. Psychologizing is inappropriately explaining or interpreting in psychological terms.

For example, a girl who went to an extremely strict Catholic school was transferred to a less stringent public school, where she was caught smoking. The therapist could have psychologized by invoking all kinds of emotional dynamics to explain it, but he instead said, "She was evaluating what she called freedom by trying to see if smoking a cigarette was possible." The mother psychologized by telling her husband, "She wants attention. You're a bad father." That may also be true, but the emphasis should be on the situation in a context—the girl was seeing what freedom was like in a less restrictive environment. The other condition may have existed but was not primary.

Therapists should concern themselves with the context and environment of an event to determine what to concentrate on. Patients get so used to psychologizing that they lose sight of what is important. Something could hit them on the nose and they would wonder if something is wrong with their egos. On the other hand, when therapists take things in stride and use psychological principles when they have to, therapy is effective.

When a therapist begins to build a case around a patient's past relationship with his mother, father, brother, or sister, the practitioner is psychologizing and the other person rightly rejects the idea. He does not want his mother involved in his life to such an extent. He is X years old. He went to school. He has had many kinds of experiences. It is true that his mother had an effect, but there are other influential factors in the person's life. Otherwise, after a while the patient may feel, "Gee, there's something wrong with this therapist. He mothers me. Wasn't there something else there?" The practitioner is smothering the patient. The therapist should stay with the person's reactions to present situations and not dig unless necessary. The therapist should work on the surface if possible, and the past should be left alone until a definite way of using it is found.

Information

Therapist Shock

Any material that shocks the therapist is a cause for investigation and should trigger questions in the practitioner's mind as to what is going on. Because it is different from her usual experience, the therapist needs to find out what causes the shock.

Paying Back Patients

When a person gives information or unconscious material, the therapist remains in debt until he makes the material useful to the patient. Either the patient or the therapist relates it to reality, or both do it together. The patient has invested in the therapist, and unless he gets a return, is going to squeeze the practitioner to get something back. The therapist owes him something. He feels cheated and becomes very angry if he does not get it.

Therapists should not trigger the unconscious to get new material unless it is necessary or useful in the current treatment context because the practitioner must always pay the person for what they give. Patients recognize when the therapist is simply curious and increase their demand for payment.

Handling Generalizations

The therapist should not ask for examples when a generalization is presented as that is challenging the patient. Very gradually, the practitioner should break up the generalization into pieces and explore each piece.

For example, when a patient said, "My wife is unfaithful," I assumed that he knew what he was talking about.

"What is it based on?" I asked. "Does she have a history of infidelity? When did you begin to feel she was unfaithful?"

"A year and a half ago."

"Tell me what happened a year and a half ago that made you feel she was unfaithful. Something must have happened to give you a clue."

All this time I was not challenging him, only asking questions so he could explain it himself. It was more important that he explain it to himself than to me. The patient may get angry with himself if he cannot explain it but at least he is not angry with me.

Slowing a Patient Down

Occasionally patients become so disturbed during treatment that they are in danger of becoming psychotic if their anxiety levels increase. At that point, therapists should slow down the treatment process. Going slow means not exposing or allowing the patient to discover any more about themselves that might increase anxiety. At that point, patients need supportive relationships to hold them together.

The therapist can also approach the situation intellectually, keeping the emotional turmoil to a minimum, by using whatever the patient gives to explain what the two of them are trying to do. This reaches a point of diminishing returns, and the patient begins to feel, "You're explaining the same stuff over and over again. I've heard you. Let's go find out something about me." The intellectual approach seems to act as a goad. The therapist may say verbally or by attitude, "Look, we're working intellectually, but there's much more there that we'll eventually get to." The patient reacts with, "Let's get on with it." At that point, the therapist must use her authority to have the patient feel she knows what she is doing and that both of them will feel when it is right to uncover and probe.

Patients continue treatment when therapists slow down because they are still learning about themselves, albeit intellectually. What happens between them and their therapists and their attempts to do what they should tells them a great deal. They become aware of how they hide, but their therapists accept them anyway. They learn what subjects they cannot stay with and the emotional limitations within which they live. This information arouses their curiosity. They wonder, "What's going to happen today? What will I find out?" This is achieved without probing or going below the surface but requires patients to become intellectually engaged.

Using Illustrations

Therapists should not draw conclusions from any anecdote told to illustrate a point. The story is an attempt to see which emotions are triggered. After knowing that, therapists can decide what to do about it. I use illustrations experimentally, not knowing beforehand what effect they will have. When therapists draw conclusions, they have assumed that their anecdotes have done certain things. The practitioners' assumptions are impositions that cue patients to defend themselves. If therapists give the patients their illustrations and leave it at that, patients may decide if the illustrations apply to them. They either react to them or let them go. When a patient asks why the therapist is telling the story, the therapist should say it is because it simply occurred to the practitioner, who must share it with the person.

Patient Leads at Beginning of Psychotherapy

The patients know more about themselves than their therapist does. Practitioners do not know very much about the patients until the patients enlighten them. Practitioners enable patients to learn about themselves and to tell them what they have learned. When therapists lead, patients do not have to give any information. Patients can just talk about whatever their therapists bring up. Therefore, therapists follow their patients' leads on what to talk about.

In any relationship in which a person wants to be of help, the therapist has to follow for a long time before she can lead. A helper needs the time to follow and learn about a person to do what is right. A therapist who leads before following implies he already knows what he needs to know. He suggests he is omniscient, and the patient feels like telling him to go to hell because she has no respect for him. Eventually the practitioner can lead, after the patient has provided enough information to suggest a direction.

In the meantime, it is important that the therapist keeps quiet and listens. A time comes when the practitioner can react intuitively, spontaneously, and a great deal of the time correctly; first, the therapist should keep his mouth shut and listen.

The Patient's Pace

Sitting and not saying a word is harder work than doing something. It calls for great self-discipline. The therapist can only do something at the patient's pace. If the patient does not go anywhere, neither can the therapist. At the end of the session, the practitioner may say, "We didn't get anywhere today because so and so. That's the way it is." This tells the patient where they are and why. Maybe next time the two of them will be able to do more. The person takes nothing away; that may make her want to try to do more the next time. I explain to patients they have to give me opportunities to work with their emotional problems.

The Therapist as a Mirror

Therapists let their patients use them the same way as they use other people, except practitioners tell patients how it feels to be used in such a way. These therapists are not revealing themselves to their patients in a personal sense. They are simply letting their patients know their reactions. The patient's behavior is a symptom to which the therapist reacts. Other people do not do this. Instead, they just want to get away from the person.

For example, an angry person needs help to examine and discover why she is verbally punching the therapist. Before entering therapy the patient's punches were mostly in fantasy. Now they are real and are opportunities for both people to look at them.

The therapist can say, "Look, this is what you did with me. How come? Why did you do it? What do you get out of it? What can we do about it? You can do it here, but if you do it outside, somebody will knock you unconscious."

Individualizing a Troubling Patient

Sometimes treatment with a person becomes a habit. The patient becomes an extension of the therapist and must be separated from the therapist. The practitioner has lost his separate, individual awareness of himself. Such an intimate therapeutic closeness may cover up much anger and hostility. When the extension is severed, the two people look at each other anew, reacting with, "I didn't know this" or "I didn't know that."

When therapists do not know how patients feel about them, they may think these persons have many attitudes and feelings that may not be there. Practitioners should ask patients how they personally feel about them. In revealing their feelings about them, patients reduce much of their practitioners' ignorance. While the situation may be worse than the therapist thought, at least she knows what she is dealing with. As the person individualizes herself, the therapist's ability to deal with her increases.

When the images the therapist and the patient have of each other get blurred because of closeness, they need to move back and refocus. The less the practitioner sees the other person, the more of an enemy the patient becomes. The unknown and the unpredictable create the therapist's fears.

THE COMING, GOING, AND GENERAL
WEARING AWAY OF PATHOLOGY

Symptom Reappearance

During treatment some symptoms and problems become like underground springs that vanish and suddenly reappear. At one time, symptoms may be very severe, then for months they do not appear. It may take as long as a year before they suddenly resurface and then go down again. Finally they come up again, but they do not go down as deeply; then they disappear.

Repetitive Behavior

Sometimes patients repeat themselves by wanting to go back to a situation they were familiar with in the past; for instance, a situation where a negative has been used long enough—or has used the patient long enough—that it becomes a positive. One of the important aspects of treatment is patient adaptability. As far as repetitive behavior is concerned, adaptability means the person has become so attached to her environment that she is an extension of it. She may have become so used to being abused, for example, that she misses it when it is not there and goes looking for abuse.

People feel alive when they experience pleasure or pain. Some people cannot enjoy pleasure and turn it into pain if they can. It is not so much that they miss the hurt, but they do not feel alive because there is no pain.

The therapist has to discover what the patient gets out of the repetition. What is the person looking for or wanting? When this is learned, the therapist can ask, "What do you need that for?"

Dealing with Compulsive Behavior

An emotional symptom is of necessity compulsive. Let us say such a symptom is suspiciousness. In that case, the person has to restrain himself from expressing the suspicion he is always feeling. The suspicion cumulates inside and congeals; that is, the person is frozen in an attitude of suspiciousness. When it is finally expressed, the symptom has behind it an accumulated charge of great force which makes it emerge compulsively.

Compulsive behavior pains patients, because they do not want to be like addicts. They feel enslaved and seek to untangle themselves. The therapist's office gives the patient a stage on which she can act out her repetitive behavior. When the patient acts it out—especially if her practitioner provides the stage, props, and some of the scenery—she can modify her compulsive behavior. The therapist must enable the patient to repeat the experience over and over again, and the patient must have an urge for this repetition even though it is painful.

The therapist conceptualizes for the patient, "This is what we are doing and this is why we are doing it, and if we do it enough there will be a modification." It has to go on and on, and the therapist has to catch this compulsion manifesting itself in all kinds of ways and plays it out from various angles.

An example of this is a patient who cannot give vent to bottled-up anger; instead she is too nice to people. The therapist gives the patient a doll named for whomever the patient is angry at. The practitioner urges the reluctant patient to throw the doll at the wall full force. The person is encouraged to do this again and again until she feels she has done it enough and gained some distance from her anger. Now she may begin to modify her method of coping with her anger.

Rationalization of Pathology

A conceptualization enables patients to control their emotions by putting experiences into understandable intellectual categories. Sometimes, however, the therapist conceptualizes the patient's behavior so that it becomes a rationalization of the patient's pathology.

The therapist may point out that the patient's situation explains his behavior. "Of course you were angry. I don't see how else you could feel under those conditions." The person sees that as an excuse for his behavior. The therapist has created a rationalization in which the patient hides, thinking, "There isn't any other way for me to feel, so there isn't any other way to behave." Although they both work with the rationalization to change the situation, nothing changes emotionally. This creates another set of conditions for repetitive behavior.

Conflict Resolution

Unresolved conflict makes a person behave repetitively. When a patient is able to talk about conflict openly, his pain is increased, creating a greater need to resolve the conflict. At first nothing is resolved. The main thing is that the process of resolution has begun. The conflict resolves itself as the patient swings back and forth like a pendulum through an arc of indecisions until finally coming to rest on one.

Fear and Conflicted Desire. Any fear a person expresses should arouse the therapist's interest, because the fear points out a conflict about something. If a patient is afraid he will lose interest in treatment, it means he is very much interested but conflicted about the interest. The interest contains within itself a distortion—like a knothole in a tree—which the therapist should examine.

A fear creating a conflicted desire has an urge or persistency worthy of examination. It usually does not look like a logical fear. The therapist should always work by opposites. The fear indicates a very strong desire that the fear is trying to eliminate.

Guilt

Therapist Absolution

Sin is not guilt. You are guilty after you have sinned, not before. When you feel guilty, you feel responsible for already having behaved badly. Sin is breaking the command of God or the rules by which you have been taught to live. You have to believe in God or these rules to feel you broke the command. You do not steal; instead, you work for a living because it has been banged into you that stealing is a sin. If I had my hand in a cash register drawer, I would pull it back for fear that someone were watching me. I am not guilty, because I have not stolen yet. But I feel sinful even before I do it, because I believe that thinking of stealing is a sin.

All of this is about anxiety. How badly will I be punished for my misdeeds? If you really accept the concept of sin, if you have a relationship with God, and if a priest absolves you from your sins, then your anxiety is reduced and you can start all over again. But if you are guilty because you sinned and if you do not know or care if there is a God, then you turn to the therapist to take care of your guilt. Either the therapist absolves you of sin or you must absolve yourself. The therapist has too much anxiety, guilt, and fear to absolve you. He too has sinned and does not have the power of absolution. So therapy becomes a dervish dance and very often fails, as the patient whirls around the therapist seeking absolution and the therapist spins in place unable to relieve the person's anxiety.

Withholding

All patients are dressed in the armor of resistance against therapists because they want to hold on to what they have. Therapists can affect patients by having them feel it is a sin to hold back material in therapy because therapists and patients are supposed to get at what is happening.

Generally, patients withhold because they have done "sinful" things in reality or fantasy, or both. Sin is the more dramatic and original way of talking about guilt. Here sin does not mean that the patient has done something that God says you should not do. Sin refers to the patient having done something unacceptable to himself or to other people.

To get to the patient's present guilts, the therapist has to touch many other sins first. At first, the patient needs to share sins to find out it is possible to talk about them and to see that the therapist accepts his sinful, guilty self. The therapist should have the patient remember and discuss all the things he has done in the past that he feels guilty about, such as stealing pennies as a child. The therapist should explain how these sins become exaggerated until the patient can look at them as an adult and put them in perspective. If this approach works, the therapist sees how past guilts are related to the present situation. Finally, when enough guilt is reduced—never fully removed—the patient tells the therapist more.

A Reason for Guilt

Emotionally disturbed people always feel guilty. They believe that their troubles result from having done something wrong or that something is wrong with them or both. They need a reason to explain their feeling guilty so they can live with the guilt. This neither reduces nor removes the guilt. It puts a frame around it so guilt cannot spread and entirely engulf the person.

Progress

The test of progress is the extent to which the following three work as one:

1. How well the person can let herself know what she is feeling.
2. How the person implements the way he feels and how it relates currently to the other areas of his life.
3. The person's daily routine, based on her understanding of herself.

The measure of the progress is in talking, feeling, and implementing. When the person talks, the therapist's questions are

1. Does he feel it?
2. Does she say it all?
3. Does he feel it as he says it?
4. What does she do about it?

Outward Signs

Sometimes the therapist and patient work for months and still see nothing happening. It is not a matter of the patient not being there or the therapist not reaching her. The person seems to hear the therapist. It is as if a stone thrown into the river makes a splash. It creates a ring that widens out of sight as it crosses the river to the other side. Months later the patient gives back what the therapist said.

Therapists must have patience and faith, because psychotherapy is a slow process in which patients integrate what they learn about themselves and their feelings before they can accept it. Except in a very crude way based on the therapist's sensitivity and experience, there is no way to tell something is happening when there are no outward signs.

Breakthrough

A breakthrough occurs when a person can see his past in a different light. Usually the therapist starts off with an intellectual idea about the patient's behavior which she calls to the person's attention. The idea must trigger emotions if it is to help the patient change.

Resistance

Resistance, like friction, is always present. It is the patient's unwillingness to become aware of some of the feelings influencing his behavior and to face the methods he uses to avoid that awareness. For one reason or another, such feelings are too painful to accept.

Awareness necessitates change, and change means overcoming the inertia of our usual way of living. Going into new behaviors or situations is dangerous. It is like finding oneself in a strange environment and not knowing the rules for survival. A person could easily get killed. The patient knows he began psychotherapy to change the way he lives and feels, but thinks, "Let's not change too much."

Therapists should start with the assumption that people in treatment do not want to tell their therapists anything. Telling their therapists is giving of themselves, and they may not be giving people. That is one of the reasons they are in trouble. Practitioners have to find out why they will not give. They may tell their therapists a lie as a substitute for what they know they should give. When patients do not want to talk about a subject, the therapists can ask them why not, thereby getting what is needed indirectly.

When a practitioner shakes up a patient she has broken the habit in which the person was living. The shake-up makes the person more antagonistic—more resistant to the therapist. The practitioner does not know until the next session which antagonisms to work with.

Resistance is usually covert, setting in after the first or second interview. At times, the patient is aware of resistance to uncovering feelings. A therapist should be wary when the patient becomes too nice and cooperative. It usually means the person is trying to put something over on the practitioner so that certain other feelings are not touched. The therapist's safest approach is to have some attributes of paranoia.

Reluctance and Resistance

Somewhere in the first few interviews the therapist should explain the difference between reluctance and resistance so that the patient does not feel guilty about not wanting to come to therapy. Reluctance is the natural feeling of not wanting to go to the dentist. Resistance is sitting in the dentist's chair and keeping your mouth closed. Reluctance is direct and very easy to find.

Resistance is subtle; it expresses itself in symptoms, in dreams, in all kinds of ways. The patient is usually unaware she is resisting, but she knows she is reluctant.

Later in treatment, reluctance is transformed into resistance because when the patient forms a relationship with the therapist, her not wanting to come to therapy triggers guilt. The guilt manifests itself in a detour and the detour expresses itself in resistance. An example of this is the punctual patient who begins habitually arriving late as painful intimate feelings are reported and then denies being late, saying there is something wrong with therapist's clock.

The patient's resistance tends to increase as the relationship with the therapist becomes closer because the person feels he can be more easily hurt and to a greater degree. The patient needs to have this resistance explained. Even in resistance, there are periods when it is no more than reluctance. The therapist can recognize the difference by the degree to which the reluctance is openly stated.

Rigidity

Rigidity is both a form of defense and a resistance. Patients defend against something they are afraid of. They might be afraid of being open because that was how they got hurt before. Their rigidity protects what was hurt when their defenses were down.

The questions the therapist should ask are, What purpose does the patient's rigidity serve? Why does he need it? Once those questions are asked, the therapist's mind is open to looking for answers that may or may not be there. The patient may need the rigidity because he is not capable of a better way of saving himself from pain.

Helping a Nontalker Talk

Most people who are rigid to a degree or who tend to retreat within themselves feel that nobody is interested in them. Why talk when whatever they say does not make any difference?

Below the surface, every person is a philosopher. Everyone has an attitude and a viewpoint about the world and how one relates to life, death, and so forth. This is a philosophy of life.

Therapists should encourage patients to express their philosophies and then restate them in terms of their emotional needs. One man I worked with was estranged from his wife but could not divorce her. His girlfriend—about whom he felt guilty—was pressing him to marry her. I said to him, "The impression I have is that you do not want to be alone. You're groping and trying to find someone to attach yourself to. The girlfriend may or may not be the right person for you, depending on how you want to live."

The patient has to feel the therapist understands him as another human being. If the practitioner talks that way, the person will add to and correct what is said. The therapist puts the patient in an intellectual and emotional context to which the person can respond. As a result, the person gives the therapist the correct context for her to work in. In other words, say you have a picture, and you are looking for a frame. The right frame helps to bring out what the picture is trying to express.

A Conscious Approach to Resistance

Many practitioners believe that because all resistance has its roots in the unconscious, the therapist has to deal with the unconscious to cope with resistance. While this may be necessary, it is more effective if the therapist starts handling resistance on the surface with the apparent unwillingness of the patient to talk intimately about herself. Unless the therapist begins by handling resistance on the surface, he faces a resistance to looking at a resistance.

Reducing patients' resistance by trying to make them aware of unconscious feelings is too painful if they are not aware they are resisting. They tend to stop treatment. Working on the surface lessens antagonism to therapists when the time comes to cope with stronger resistance to uncovering emotional pathology.

As long as the therapist stays on the surface and does not deal with the unconscious, she may tell the patient when she is resisting. The purpose is to discover what the patient does with the feelings she is unable to express directly. An example of this is the patient who was asked what made it hard for him to look at his feelings. Tape recorder playback brought out his avoidance to looking at his feeling by shifting to many other subjects. We discovered that he felt staying with one subject would reveal too much about him.

The therapist may deal with resistance on the surface using retrospective awareness. She asks the patient to think about a past situation similar to the present and explain how he handled it then. Does that give him any ideas for handling the present situation? Would he handle it the same way now? The patient may become aware of feelings from the past preventing him from coping with the present situation.

One resistance can be dealt with more effectively consciously. It is a conscious evasive strategy that is different for each patient. Some alcoholics admit they are continuing to drink only if the therapist asks in a very concrete, specific way:

"Have you had any alcohol?"

"No." (To themselves: "I'm going to answer that as if he means today.")

"Did you have any alcohol during this past week?"

"Yes."

Handling Resistance

1. Where possible, the therapist should conceptualize the resistance in the context of the whole case, not in a current particular situation or interview. For example, a man who had been afraid of women most of his life started to question his need for therapy. I explained his resistance as a resentment for no longer finding pleasure in his pathological behavior. He had been masturbating frequently and could no longer do this, but he was not as afraid of women and got a more satisfying sexual pleasure from them.

Patients resent therapy as they are getting better because they lose their pathological pleasure. If the therapist can help the patient to get a rough idea of how the person's pathological pleasure was converted to healthy pleasure, the resistance is reduced.

2. The patient is responsible for finding the source or sources of the resistance. When the therapist says he is stopped, he is reinforcing the patient's negativism. Deep down the patient feels, "See, I got to that guy. See, he thinks he's a smart guy, but I'm

smarter. I'll make him squirm." The therapist should point out how the patient's behavior is stopping progress: "This, patient, is what you did or didn't do to keep us from making any further progress."

3. The therapist should keep the patient glued to the reality of the present and interpret openly what is happening on the surface, in the here and now. When the therapist or patient interprets in terms of unconscious feelings, both of them get lost in speculation, enabling the person to hide from awareness. If the patient gives any unconscious material, the therapist should simplify it and put it in a concrete context so that the person does not take the two of them off the track. They should not get involved in interpretations of unconscious feelings in which, for example, the patient is like her father, mother, grandfather, or whatever.

4. This approach to resistance is a wedge to crack open character armor. There is a tendency on the part of the patient and therapist to dissipate the impact of the approach through too much interpretation or by bringing in too much material to explain the resistance. Dissipating gives the patient the chance he is looking for to run from awareness. Never mind associations to father, mother, grandfather, or trying to cover a lot of ground. Keep it short.

5. The therapist should not call a psychological phenomenon by its name, but describe it. For example, after the resistance has been spelled out, if the therapist wants to give it a name, fine. Naming the resistance at the beginning enables the patient to enlarge upon it and hide in the name.

Stopping in Midtreatment

Occasionally the therapist, with the agreement of the patient, has to suspend therapy. I call it putting the patient on vacation. This can happen at any time in treatment.

Patient Unable to Go Further

At times the patient's resistance is so great that it appears she has gone as far as she can go. The therapist can describe the two of them as having done a very good paint job, but there are still termites they were not able to get at because the patient is not yet ready. The word *termites* is used here as a symbol for unconscious feelings. Both termites and feelings work imperceptibly in the dark, the insects on the foundations of a house, the feelings on a person. An indication of termites is finding small piles of sawdust on the ground around the house. With emotional termites, the patient sees himself having feelings or behaving in destructive ways he does not understand. Neither the therapist nor patient knows when the termites will begin to operate again; when they do, the patient may have to return to treatment with a good chance of lessened resistance. Meanwhile, the patient and therapist have a connection in absentia.

Partial Therapy

Other times therapy is more effective when it is done in parts. These patients need an absence from therapy to experience what they have talked about and become aware of. It takes time for them to emotionally and intellectually assimilate the material. They get a glimpse of what else needs to be dealt with and reenter treatment to further resolve their emotional problems.

A Temporary Stop

One effect of psychotherapy is that it tranquilizes people to the extent that they are able to live with bad situations. Alleviation of the patient's upset perpetuates the status quo. The end result is confused patients who thought they knew what was going on but do not understand why things have not gotten better. I explain to them how I see their situation. I tell them that it is better for them to be on their own for a while just to experience what is going on and determine if conditions are as they think. When they are ready, we can meet again and discuss what they saw. Turning a chronic state into an acute one makes them amenable to treatment. The increase in pain makes patients more aware of the situation and motivated to do something.

Band-Aid Approach

For some people a band-aid job is enough. Trying to do more than that would open up all kinds of psychic wounds and disturb emotional balances that the therapist cannot improve on. A band-aid job enables the person to cope with a current situation without uncovering any more of the troubling feelings and emotions than is absolutely necessary. This leaves the door open for the patient to return when she wants, after having dealt with her problems on a localized basis.

Using interventions in a band-aid situation makes the person more apt to run into his own resistance. The fact that he can do so little indicates to him that that is as much as he can do and he is willing to stop treatment.

THE NIGHTMARE OF ANXIETY OR CHANGE

Throughout treatment therapists must cope with patients' anxiety. It fuels patients' resistance to change because they fear hurt will overwhelm and destroy them. In a changed situation, patients no longer know what pain to expect or how to protect themselves against it. They feel exposed and to some extent helpless. They have not tested themselves in the new situation and tend to underestimate what they can tolerate. Although patients have progressed to a more satisfying way of living, the fear of death is never far away. The old way is dying and the new is just emerging.

Understanding something enables people to direct it to some degree. Control is synonymous with understanding. If people can begin to understand their anxiety, they can begin to cope with it. This section describes the different kinds of anxiety and how they may be approached.

Anxiety

No one knows what anxiety in any of its three forms—basic, neurotic, and natural—is, but something is known about what it does. It leaves one afraid and unable to lessen or get rid of the fear. It wears down and destroys a person's life because it keeps him on a perpetual alert. All human anxiety is derived from basic anxiety, the awareness and fear of death. Neurotic anxiety is based on imaginary fears that the person thinks might kill her. Natural anxiety is based on realistic fears of being destroyed.

Anxiety is the difficulty of living experienced through feelings instead of thinking about it. Intense anxiety prevents thinking about the difficulty so one can see what to do. People in a state of anxiety are on the boundary line between life and death. They are as much aware of death as they are of life and do not know where they are. Many times a person wants to commit suicide simply to gain relief from anxiety: being dead is better than being afraid of dying. The anxiety is over.

Conflicts are a major source of anxiety. Anxiety is triggered when people do not know which way to turn. The conflict is based on the inability to make any choice because they are afraid they cannot handle what might happen no matter which way they go. The anxiety increases as the severity of the conflict increases; patients become panicky. If they can find a way out or decide on something to do, the panic decreases. Many conflicts cannot be resolved because conflict and life are inseparable. The best one can do is to be anxious but go on living as a reprieve from death.

Life, at times, appears stupid, foolish, absurd, nonsensical, and unpredictable, making anxiety inevitable. People are aware of how contradictory life is. Anxiety results from an accentuation of the contradictions while people are trying not to be aware of them.

An anxious patient who comes to a therapist is like a filled vacuum cleaner dust bag that needs to be emptied. Emptying means the patient talks to the therapist about what bothers her in a way she cannot talk with anyone else. This makes room in the dust bag so it does not burst. Bursting means psychosis. The bag will fill again, but the therapist has temporarily gotten rid of enough dust that the patient can keep going. The anxiety will return; meanwhile, the person has found a more comfortable way to live.

The Crux of Any Emotional Problem

Humans are not Homo Sapiens—knowing, wise, sage. We are ignorant and frequently react to life with a great deal of fear. An emotional problem is always a confused, fearful reaction to a reality the patient feels will destroy him. This confused fear is the indication of anxiety; therefore, anxiety is the crux of any emotional problem.

General Approach to Anxiety

Psychotherapy behaves as a problem-solving discipline helping people to find solutions. It assumes that therapists know enough about how human beings work emotionally so that, using psychological knowledge, patients' emotional problems can be solved. It assumes that therapists know what anxiety is and can resolve it. None of this is correct.

Anxiety is not solvable. Like breathing or life, it is always there. Basic anxiety and, therefore, all anxiety is concerned with finding the meaning of life so that death can be faced. Anxiety can be coped with but not cured because death cannot be negated.

For most of their lives people defy death by behaving as if they are going to live forever. Such denial is a part of everyday life. The difficulties encountered in disturbed behavior are based, to a great extent, on too much denial. The therapist has to become aware of and understand what patients need to deny. As the therapist talks about it, patients learn to accept what they are denying.

Therapists have to sense as soon as possible what the anxious patient is trying to say. Once the therapist knows, it is not necessary to let the patient know logically. The patient senses the therapist knows and is no longer as fearful. Not only is the patient no longer alone with the anxiety, but the two of them are actually coping with it as well.

The therapist has to realize anxiety is a given in life, never to be gotten rid of. The patient may relate to it a little better if she, too, is aware of this. The person may feel, "I wish it weren't so. I don't like anxiety but I'll have to live with it." When that happens, it lessens the pressures the patient feels in life because both she and the therapist are no longer making demands that they get rid of anxiety, only lessen it. It enables the therapist to work with less anxiety.

The therapist must distinguish between natural, neurotic, and basic anxiety. Determining the different fears helps people to cope with real fears and to eliminate imaginary fears. Patients get so mixed up that they do not know which is which. Clarifying people's fears reduces their anxieties and enables them to focus on the resolvable problems.

Handling Anxiety

The working definition of anxiety is unknown fear. When the therapist changes this to a known fear, the patient can see what to do to either reduce or get rid of it. The therapist has to look for what the patient thinks will destroy him. Therapists have to guess at it because patients deny that anything can wipe them out. As the therapist talks about it, whatever the patient thinks can annihilate him is reduced in intensity and force. This frees the patient to find a less anxiety-ridden situation.

Treating Basic Anxiety

Basic anxiety is a given because there is life and there is death and we know nothing about either. We do not know where we came from or where we are going. The only thing we know about is that limited area between life and death called consciousness. Life and death are frustrations because there is not enough time in between for people to realize what they really want. When the frustration becomes too intense, a feeling of futility creates anxiety. Patients say, "I am helpless to do anything satisfying and meaningful with my life. I am at the mercy of chance."

Basic anxiety is found at all ages but is most prevalent among retired people, because they think about dying all the time. Prior to retirement, they were so busy doing something they did not have time to dwell on death.

In a state of basic anxiety patients are so aware and afraid of dying that they want to die to escape the fear. Basic anxiety cannot be cured or reduced, so the therapists try to help patients understand it. If they do, the patients can try to help themselves. The only way patients can tranquilize basic anxiety—which is all that can be done—is to keep busy through some form of art or occupation in which they are creative. If people can express themselves enough, they can cope with the difficulties of basic anxiety without needing medication.

Neurotic Anxiety

Neurotic anxiety is the anticipation of the catastrophe that has not yet occurred. It is being afraid of being afraid because these people know fear makes them create horrifying imaginary situations. Because life is not predictable, the catastrophe might occur. There is an element of truth in all neurotic anxiety. One may be killed crossing a busy street if someone drives through a red light. This does not mean one should stay on the curb, forever unable to cross the street. Thus there is a valid basis for neurotic anxiety, but it is an overexaggerred fear. The therapist explains that those fears are imaginary, but they could happen, too. It is as though patients are trying to prepare themselves in case these fears come true. Everybody lives this way to some extent.

Imagining the Worst

This approach is used when the therapist is unable to reduce anxiety by changing the unknown fear to a known fear. When the therapist uses the patient's imagination to create the worst possible thing that can happen, it is as if it has already happened. For example, if you are afraid of breaking a leg and imagine the experience, you have faced the fear in your imagination.

The therapist starts by saying, "Look, I'm going to present you with certain situations and you've got to imagine that you're there and react as though they're real. Alright? Tell me, what's the greatest fear you have at night? What would be the greatest fear that would come to your mind?" The patient tells of neurotic fears the practitioner probably did not know the person had. The therapist then uses one of those fears to describe a situation in which the patient is threatened now. The person experiences a tremendous increase of anxiety, and he is asked to rescue himself.

For example, the therapist describes the person caught in a crowded movie house full of smoke and fire. There is only one small exit. People are trampling each other in panic. The patient cannot get out and will choke to death in a matter of minutes. The person does not have much longer to live. Then the patient is asked to come up with a way to save himself and does. Until the crush at the exit is relieved, he lays on the floor under the theater seats where there is air and people cannot step on him. As the patient imagines this scene, his anxiety should increase enormously. After the patient gets out of the situation, the therapist clarifies what she is trying to do.

The therapist explains she is trying to create a life or death situation that captures the patient's emotional state. For a long time, the person has felt as if he were fighting for his life, living in a state of anxiety. As far as the patient is concerned, that fire was reality. He emerged from the danger, saved. Now he knows anxiety can be dealt with if it is faced because he did face it. All this the therapist explains to the patient after the experience. The therapist went to the patient's imagination and experience and made him find a way to reduce the anxiety. The person now feels able to try to do the same thing with the conflict in reality.

The therapist creates situations in which the neurotic fear becomes exaggerated imaginatively. The patient learns that some of the anxiety is unreal, which can only happen by experiencing the imagined fear. The therapist continues to improvise anxiety-provoking situations until the patient firmly grasps that some of his anxiety is imaginary fear.

The therapist is trying to give the person some control over anxiety. It will come back again and again, but the patient is being helped to deal with it each time. The patient who feels some control over it gets a respite in which to think about the anxiety and see what to do. Therapy, when successful, consists of creating distance and choice.

Other Ways of Reducing Anxiety

Overwhelmed by an Emotion

Many children and adults are overwhelmed by an emotion for two reasons: (1) they may have never experienced the emotion before or (2) they do not have the words to express the emotion. They are overwhelmed by the emotion because they cannot contain it. The therapist should talk about the emotion, in the process giving patients the words and ideas they need. A patient overwhelmed by an emotion is unable to find the words that organize it. These people use all kinds of words, but never ones that have any clear meaning.

Emotionally disturbed people are undisciplined. The therapist does not discipline but by using words in the patient's context creates a situation where the emotional energy is redirected. The person can look at what happened by using the words. Let us say that emotion is an urge that propels a person in a certain direction. In that sense we can find emotions in the taste buds. The doctor may say, "Don't eat pickles or you'll get a bellyache," but the patient has the urge to eat them. Every time she eats pickles she gets a bellyache. She soon realizes she can either stop eating them or have a bellyache. The urge to have a pickle is caught by the words, "Don't eat it or you'll have a bellyache." The person is no longer overwhelmed by the emotion as it is organized by her use of words and contained.

Distancing

A therapist asks a patient to notice if during anxiety attacks she has particular emotions, feelings, or fears. If so, the patient is to catch them, remember them, and report them. These things observed acquire the feel of foreign bodies in a person's emotional organization. In this way the patient puts distance between herself and the anxiety attacks, preventing herself from becoming overwhelmed. The therapist is trying to create distance all the time.

Pictorializing Anxiety

The therapist first talks with the patient about anxiety by trying to discover a situation in which the person felt her life was in danger. When the person puts herself back into that situation and that feeling, that is anxiety. While in the past situation, the therapist should ask her, "What happened there? What did you imagine then? What did you try to do? What did you not try to do?" Then the therapist explains they are dealing with a similar feeling, not situation, now. This is trying to concretize the anxiety so the patient knows what she has and how she is going to deal with it.

Bringing the patient up to the present, the therapist asks her to visualize the current anxiety: "Can you portray what you are feeling now as a picture?" The therapist explains this is because there is no such thing as free-floating emotion; it needs to connect to something. To help it hook up, the patient creates visual images. When the patient has a picture, the therapist asks her to change the picture so that she no longer feels threatened. This approach lets the patient see she has handled anxiety before. She can concretize it and project it like a movie whose scenes she can change and therefore deal with again.

I AM

Regression, after it occurs, can be measured rather accurately. During a regression the patient goes back to the way he behaved when he was younger and tries to deal with the early pathologies that treatment has brought to the fore. A regression has a pleasurable component. A person frustrated at the age of 42 may go back to an earlier age where he contended with life on a less mature level but felt good about it. It is not difficult to discover how far back the person has regressed chronologically.

Sometimes patients have to regress before they can be helped. Then the patients tell their therapists that they realize things they never were aware of before. For perhaps the first time in their lives patients are conscious of themselves. It is an early sign of an emerging self. This awareness is progress in spite of the regression. Therapists must explain this so patients know that they are making progress while regressing. This helps people remain in treatment. Regression may also so discourage patients that they become depressed and need the awareness of progress to come out of it.

As treatment proceeds, the self that was buried under many impositions begins to emerge. The person becomes aware of emotions and feelings and begins to divest herself of the lifestyles, values, conditionings, and imitations of others that were imposed on her. The patient decides, mostly unconsciously, what she will use from others to define herself and what she will let go. Symbolically the patient rejects all the meaningful people in her life who were role models, assimilating from them only that which enables her to enter the drama of her life on her own terms.

As this begins to happen, the therapist explains to the patient, "You were born into a family. You looked to your mother to learn how you should be as a woman. You didn't have enough life experience to know how you wanted to live or what was important to you, so you adopted your parents' lifestyle. They, your teachers, friends, and the environment you grew up in, imposed their values on you, and you accepted them as a matter of convenience. As you grew up, you realized that parts of you were at odds with what you had been led to believe was the right way to live. You wanted to live differently, but all kinds of fears stopped you. We are uncovering those fears and are either lessening or getting rid of them so they no longer hold you back. Now we are learning how you really want to live."

The psychic self which emerges will be stained as a result of its previous experiences and relationships. It will have to be cleansed of uncharacteristic attitudes and behaviors. Having had a glimpse of what was characteristic of the person, the therapist may have a rough idea of what may emerge in its place. However, some uncharacteristic expression will always remain. During this time, the patient needs great emotional support as that which was always there makes its entrance.

SOME TREATMENT AIMS

Treatment and Meaning

Treatment helps patients to look at and understand their experiences. They learn what they should or should not have done. The job of the therapist is to help them to look, not to give patients whatever wisdom he may have.

Treatment helps patients find out what has the greatest meaning to them. Life, movement, the way a person sits, everything has a meaning. Therapists have to find meaning in persons' everyday material and help them see it. Patients then organize their lives around whatever they see that has the greatest meaning to them.

Inferences

A great part of the therapist's work consists of inferences. The meaning of a fact is more important than the fact itself. From any one experience a number of meanings can be inferred based on context, age, or previous experience. The therapist can do two things with the patient's experiences: He can say he does not know what they mean and mentally file them away and wait for understanding. Otherwise, the therapist has an idea of what the experience means to the patient and acts on that basis while leaving the way open for additional meaning to come.

For example, these are two inferences that can be made from symptoms:

1. Guessing or knowing what brought on the symptoms enables the therapist to predict how the patient will behave in the present when a similar situation appears.

2. Knowing how a symptom affects both the patient and therapist gives them an idea of the problems the symptom creates.

Treatment and Awareness

A neurotic is the essence of conflict, and conflict is synonymous with indecision. The aim of treatment is to enable patients to make decisions based on their awareness of what is happening to them emotionally. One of the problems of treating a neurotic is the intellectual awareness which accentuates the conflict. Most severe neurotics are extremely intelligent and intellectual. They have the words, ideas, knowledge, and ability to think about themselves. This reinforces their tendency to think about their emotions and feelings instead of experiencing them. The nucleus of a neurotic problem is this excessive intellectual awareness of emotions and feelings which psychotherapy further emphasizes to help these people.

Awareness is not always a good thing. People need just enough awareness to survive in the present. Their own need for continued survival will guide them from that point on.

Adaptation

Neurotic behavior is a way of bypassing emotions so one can live a life of conformity without being troubled—in other words, trying to live life unaffected by feelings. The neurotic cannot be cured because a basic unresolvable conflict between emotion and intellect is embedded in human beings. It is as though intellect and emotion are two different unrelated systems. The emotions react to the apprehension of a situation and seek an outlet in action as soon as possible. The intellect reacts to an accumulation of facts acquired piece by piece, sees many possibilities arising from any action, ruminates, and acts deliberately. The emotions override the intellect, triggering action without thought. The intellect prevents any spontaneous emotional reaction. One tends to cancel out the other. An example of this is the problem of anxiety. Based on previous experience, patients know that if they can face what they are afraid of, they are on the road to coping with the fear. However, the fear carries with it such a strong connotation of danger these people feel they will die if they confront it. The result is a deadlock, an anxiety attack.

A neurotic problem is incurable because therapists do not know how to reconcile emotion and intellect. Here cure means the removal of the conflict which prevents people from acting on their emotions and feelings in unison with their intellects. Usually the conflict is encapsulated. Encapsulation means the ability to deny emotions and feelings by believing they do not exist. The aim of therapy then becomes adaptation, enabling the patient to use whatever is available to cope with life, to bypass difficulties instead of becoming involved in them. In an adaptation the encapsulation is dissolved; there is a conscious realization of the problem and some feeling or understanding of the unconscious mechanisms involved.

Some Treatment Aims

Emotional pressure is an integral part of human life. Low tolerance to emotional pressure comes from one's heredity or being stuck at an earlier stage of emotional development. Either of these may lead to a pathology common to all the members of a family; it may express itself through different symptoms. An emotional problem is made evident by poorly controlled behavior out of context. This is exemplified by the person who is intellectually brilliant and emotionally stupid or who is outwardly rigid but unpredictably explosive.

Character therapy can deal with neurotic behavior and defines it as emotional strangulation by unresolved traumas, characterized by unpredictable destructive emotional eruptions. Psychosis, fainting, and suicide are attempts to escape from the neurotic problem, the therapist, and treatment. Such efforts indicate treatment failure. In part, these attempts are explosions triggered by the patient's inadequate coping with emotional pressures. Psychotherapy is to neurosis and emotional problems what insulin is to diabetes. The pathology is controlled, not cured.

Some treatment aims are:

1. Reducing anxiety by changing it to known fears and dealing with those fears. In the process, the therapist should separate imaginary neurotic fear from real fear.

A trauma is an emotional experience that the nervous system, the self, cannot assimilate. It is as if a piece of food got stuck in the throat and interfered with breathing. It creates many symptoms, the foremost of which is anxiety. Treatment helps to assimilate the trauma and thereby reduces the anxiety.

Treatment enables people to become aware of contradictions in their lives with which they cannot live. They cannot decide which way they want to go, creating much anxiety. With further treatment, patients make choices and reduce their anxiety.

2. Teaching people to regulate the pressure of their emotions as they would the air in a tire. Patients realize they need to find ways to express their emotions and feelings so that they do not build up and overwhelm them.

3. Helping patients to become aware of the difference between hostility and anger so patients can understand who or what they are angry about and cope with it.

4. Redirecting displaced emotions to their original source and resolving them.

5. Helping patients to have enough distance from their emotions and feelings that they can think and exercise choice.

6. Changing psychic pain into suffering by giving it meaning.

7. Converting pathological pleasure to healthy pleasure. Nobody knows how the conversion of pathological pleasure to healthy pleasure takes place. The general approach in treatment is to concentrate on the person's pathology, ignoring their healthy aspects. The therapist should call patients' attention to the positive that is actually manifested and not infer it. For patients, finding something positive is like getting a gold star from the teacher. The effect is cumulative, and they come to prefer the pleasure they get from healthy behavior. This is my guess as to how the conversion takes place.

Untreated emotional problems mean a life lived destructively; successful treatment means living life constructively.

Discharge

There are three criteria for discharging a patient. First of all, the patient feels ready for discharge. In spite of fear and trepidation she wants to try to handle things on her own. Second, treatment has prepared her for discharge because she is increasingly making and implementing choices. Most of the time she is making choices good for her. Some errors happen, but they are not calamitous. Third, there is a likelihood that some pathological behavior will return. The therapist will need to discriminate if it is acting out or a behavior problem. Acting out means the patient is still frustrated in expressing herself and should not be discharged. In a behavior problem, the patient knows she is engaging in pathological behavior to scare the therapist into keeping her in therapy. In such a case, the therapist should discharge the patient.

At the end of treatment I hope my patients have many problems and tell them so. It means they are engaged in living, which is always problematical. They will cope with the problems and make the right choices based on what they learned about themselves in therapy. If at any time they do not know what to do, they know they can return for help in getting over a rough spot.

NOTES

1. Henri Bergson, *Time and Free Will*, Harper Torchbooks, The Academy Library (New York: Harper and Row, 1960), p. 100.

2. Ibid., *The Creative Mind, An Introduction to Metaphysics*, The Wisdom Library (New York: Philosophical Library, 1946), p. 179.

Bibliography

Bergson, Henri. *Creative Evolution*. Translated by Arthur Mitchell. The Modern Library. New York: Random House, 1944.

Bergson, Henri. *The Creative Mind, An Introduction to Metaphysics*. The Wisdom Library. New York: Philosophical Library, 1946.

Bergson, Henri. *Time and Free Will*. Harper Torchbooks, The Academy Library. New York: Harper and Row, 1960.

Chaplin, J. P. *Dictionary of Psychology*. Revised edition, Laurel Editions. New York: Dell, 1984.

Freud, Sigmund. "Analysis, Terminable and Interminable." In *Collected Papers*, Vol. 5. New York: Basic Books, 1959.

James, William. *Pragmatism and Other Essays*. New York: Washington Square Press, 1963.

Montaigne, Michel de. *Montaigne Selected Essays*. Translated by Charles Colton and William Hazlett. The Modern Library. New York: Random House, 1949.

Reich, Wilhelm. *Character Analysis*. 3d enlarged edition. Translated by Theodore P. Wolfe. The Noonday Press. New York: Farrar, Straus and Giroux, 1969.

Sinnott, Edmund W. *Cell and Psyche, The Biology of Purpose*. Harper Torchbooks/The Science Library. New York: Harper Brothers, 1961.

Webster's Third New International Dictionary of the English Language Unabridged. Springfield, MA: G & C Merriam Company, 1963.

Index

About the Author

JULES MEISLER is a psychotherapist in private practice in Thousand Oaks, California.